RICHARD STONE

QUANTITY
AND
PRICE INDEXES
IN NATIONAL ACCOUNTS

PUBLISHED BY
THE ORGANISATION FOR EUROPEAN ECONOMIC CO-OPERATION
2, rue André-Pascal, Paris · 16e

The Organisation for European Economic Co-operation comprises the following Member countries: Austria, Belgium, Denmark, France, Germany, Greece, Iceland, Ireland, Italy, Luxembourg, the Netherlands, Norway, Portugal, Sweden, Switzerland, Turkey and the United Kingdom. The Organisation came into being with the signing of the Convention for European Economic Co-operation on 16th April 1948, when Member Governments pledged themselves "to combine their economic strength, to join together to make the fullest collective use of their individual capacities and potentialities, to increase their production, develop and modernise their industrial and agricultural equipment, expand their commerce, reduce progressively barriers to trade among themselves, promote full employment and restore or maintain the stability of their economies and general confidence in their national currencies". Representatives of each of the Member countries meet daily at O.E.E.C.'s headquarters, the Château de la Muette, Paris, to discuss their economic problems and work out common solutions. The United States and Canada, although not members of the Organisation, participate in its work and Yugoslavia is represented by an observer. Spain participates as a full member in the work of the agricultural bodies of the Organisation.

Published in November 1956

CONTENTS

FOREWORD 7

I. THE REPORT AND ITS BACKGROUND 9
    1. The purpose of the Report 9
    2. Different aspects of the problem of index-numbers 11
    3. The arrangement of the Report 14

II. INDEX-NUMBERS AND ECONOMIC THEORY 17
    1. Index-numbers from the consumer's point of view 17
    2. An example: the linear expenditure system 19
    3. Index-numbers from the producer's point of view 21
    4. Practical possibilities 22
    5. The valuation of commodities 24

III. INDEX-NUMBERS IN A SOCIAL ACCOUNTING FRAMEWORK 27
    1. The production boundary 27
    2. An extension of the Standardised System 30
    3. Commodity flows in the production accounts 33
    4. Gross and net concepts 35
    5. The characteristics of aggregate index-numbers 37
    6. The application of the index-numbers to a system of commodity flows 39
    7. Market prices and factor costs 44

IV. COMMODITIES, QUANTITY UNITS AND QUALITY DIFFERENCES 47
    1. The objects of commodity transactions 47
    2. Quality variations and variety changes 48
    3. An example of the relationship of price to quality 53
    4. Other applications and a comparison with other methods 55
    5. New models and new products 57
    6. Charges which are not proportional to quantity 59

V. INTERMEDIATE SERVICES AND ROUTING PROBLEMS 61
    1. Differential prices and intermediate services 61
    2. The routing of commodity flows 63
    3. Partial comparisons 68

VI. SEASONAL VARIATIONS 73
    1. Introduction 73
    2. The treatment of seasonal commodities 74
    3. A method of seasonal adjustment 77
    4. An application of the method 83
    5. Extensions and developments 85
    6. The combination of seasonal chains 87

VII. THE TREATMENT OF NON-COMMODITY FLOWS 89
    1. The treatment of aggregates which are not entirely composed of
        commodity flows 89
    2. The arbitrary nature of attempts to balance an accounting system in
        real terms 90
    3. Various measures of the national income at constant prices ... 94
    4. Alternative concepts of non-commodity flow sat constant prices ... 95

5

VIII. GENERAL PROBLEMS OF MEASUREMENT 97

    1. Introduction 97
    2. The selection of indicators 97
    3. Alternative indicators of prices and quantities 99
    4. Short-period indicators 102
    5. Weighting 104
    6. The choice of base period 106

 IX. FAMILIAR TYPES OF INDEX-NUMBERS AND THE SYSTEM PRESENTED HERE 109

    1. Index-numbers in common use and their relationship to those
       described in this Report 109
    2. Alternative methods of reducing the money value of the domestic
       product to terms of constant prices 111
    3. Still simpler short-cut methods 112

  X. SUMMARY AND CONCLUSIONS 115
A LIST OF WORKS CITED 119

FOREWORD

The *Standardised System of National Accounts,* issued by this Organisation in 1952, was the first of a projected series of publications relating to problems which arise in social accounting. These reports are intended to provide guidance on various conceptual questions and also to set out a system of definitions and classifications of general applicability, to indicate detail that is generally desirable for analytical purposes and to provide a framework for assembling the data of various countries on a comparable basis.

The present Report carries the systematic examination of conceptual problems, which in the *Standardised System* remained confined to problems connected with the national accounts expressed in current money terms, one stage further. It deals with the problem of making comparisons between the accounts of successive periods in such a way that they are free, as far as possible, from the effect of changing prices and with the related problem of measuring and comparing the associated price movements in different parts of the economy. Such comparisons can be achieved through the construction of price and quantity index numbers on a systematic and co-ordinated plan.

The Report has two main features. First, it reviews the problems of index-number construction against the background of the social accounts as a whole and so brings out the numerous problems involved in attaining various kinds of consistency. Second, it lays stress on the need for more empirical knowledge about the factors responsible for price differences among superficially similar commodities as the basis for the establishment of better units of measurement and more reliable comparisons.

The Report was prepared by Professor Richard Stone in his capacity as a Consultant to the Organisation. A first draft was thoroughly discussed by national accounts experts of Member countries and international organisations participating in the 1952 O.E.E.C. National Accounts Conference. A revised draft taking account of the discussion at that Conference was then prepared and this in turn was submitted to the 1955 O.E.E.C. National Accounts Conference. Insofar as possible, the suggestions made by this meeting of experts are incorporated in the present text.

While a considerable degree of agreement on concepts and methods emerged from the two conferences which dealt with this subject, it was concluded that opinion and practice had not yet reached the point which would make the adoption of international standards practicable. Consequently, the Report should be regarded as a first step intended as a guide to those engaged in practical work. In view of the importance of the subject, however, it is hoped that when more experience has been gained with the practical application of the principles outlined in this Report, it will be possible to reach more formal agreement on the standards to be used in this field.

MILTON GILBERT,
Director of Economics and Statistics

8

I

THE REPORT AND ITS BACKGROUND

1. THE PURPOSE OF THE REPORT

This Report is a sequel to *A Standardised System of National Accounts* [15] and is concerned with the many problems, conceptual and practical, of comparing the entries in two or more uniform sets of social accounts relating to a single country at different periods. In one sense such comparisons are very simple; it is always possible to say that a particular entry expressed in current money terms in one period is so much larger or smaller than the corresponding entry, also expressed in current money terms, of another. Such comparisons, however, have only a limited interest because the units in which they are expressed are not uniform. The pound note of 1955 may look similar to the pound note of 1938 but in terms of what it will buy it is quite different.

The problem of establishing a more satisfactory unit can be approached by inquiring into what has happened to the value of money between the two periods to be compared. It then becomes obvious that this question is meaningless unless some standard of value is proposed. It might be suggested that the value of money should be defined in terms of its purchasing power over a gold bar of precisely defined characteristics but this would only shift the problem from the unit of currency to the bar of gold. A more illuminating approach would be to fix the definition of purchasing power in terms of a given collection of commodities the composition of which is in some sense relevant and interesting for the purpose in hand. This approach leads directly to the construction of price index-numbers.

If the two money totals to be compared represent the value of similar commodities actually bought, for example if they represent expenditure on food at two different dates, then the problem may be approached by inquiring into what has happened to the quantity of food bought between the first period and the second. But there is no obvious single unit in terms of which the quantity of food in general can be expressed. It might be suggested that the unit should be the ton or the calory. But these units would be of limited interest since neither characteristic, weight or calory content, provides a complete specification of foods. Moreover if the example had been clothing rather than foodstuffs no convenient

9

simple unit like calories would have been available. Finally if calory content were the only characteristic of different foods to be considered it would be difficult to understand why the more expensive varieties in terms of cost per calory should ever be produced or bought. Clearly there must be more in food than calories. It may not be altogether clear what characteristics are valued but at least it is possible to accept the actual values of a given period and to use these in making a weighted average of the quantity movements of the component foodstuffs between the two periods to be compared. This approach leads directly to the construction of quantity index-numbers.

These two activities, the construction of price index-numbers and the construction of quantity index-numbers, can be regarded as quite separate operations. This in fact is often done. Thus, to take two common examples, many countries publish officially an index of retail prices and an index of industrial production. The first is a form of price index-number which is of great practical utility even if there are no corresponding series of consumers' expenditure in real or money terms. The second is a form of quantity index-number which is also useful even if there are no corresponding series of total value added in industrial activity or of value added per unit of output.

Reflection will show however that the two types of index-number are complementary and that similar problems are involved in the construction of each. For example most commodities are not homogeneous and cannot be satisfactorily characterised by a single, simple, measure of quantity. But in the absence of a satisfactory unit of quantity it is not possible to derive a satisfactory price series but only a series of the average value of the heterogeneous varieties whose prices are actually recorded. Thus the existence of quality differences and changes affects both types of measurement and the same is true of most of the other problems which are encountered in this field.

With the development of national accounting and its extension to include an input-output table of commodity flows between industries within a wider social accounting framework, it becomes desirable to view the operations of constructing price and quantity index-numbers from a more comprehensive point of view. The value of a series of national accounts for successive years is severely limited if it is not combined with price and quantity information which enables the various entries to be expressed at constant prices and the associated price movements to be measured. Since an important aspect of any accounting system is the coherent arrangement of a large mass of detailed information so that what is interesting and relevant in that information can be assimilated, it is desirable that a similar coherence should be preserved in the construction of price and quantity index-numbers which are to be used in association with a system of national accounts.

Index-numbers of prices and quantities provide a means of comparing two situations with the aid of information on the prices and quantities of commodities produced, consumed and put to stock in each of them. For each entry composed of expenditure on commodities, such as consumers' expenditure on goods and services, it is possible, in principle, to construct a price and a quantity index by reference to the constituent commodities. The price index represents, in a sense to be defined precisely, the average price movement of the constituent commodities between the two dates to be compared and the quantity index represents the corresponding average quantity movement. In this Report the problem of constructing price and quantity index-numbers is considered from the point of view of attempting to construct one of each for each commodity flow in the accounting system. This approach ensures attention to the problems of achieving consistency and coherence in a system of index-numbers and provides a means of organising the discussion of the many conceptual and practical difficulties to which the subject gives rise. In practice, of course, it is not necessary that all the constituent index-numbers should be constructed but if the work is carried out on the lines suggested here the resulting index-numbers will be clearly related to one another in terms of the categories of the accounting system.

For the purpose of this Report, commodity (or product) flows are defined as all flows of goods and services other than the services of the factors of production. The exclusion of ultimate inputs into the productive system is made because of the special conceptual difficulties of attaching price and quantity measures to them. A treatment of the subject of productivity would require that these difficulties should be overcome but this complex subject must be left for separate treatment.

The non-commodity flows in the accounting system cannot, in the nature of the case, possess their own price and quantity measures in the sense in which these can be constructed for commodity flows. Consequently if they are also to be expressed, in some sense, in real terms this can only be done by reference to the price movement of a specified commodity total. In general this commodity total cannot be uniquely defined and a choice among the possibilities available must be made by the investigator for the purpose in hand. Thus in an analysis of the disposal of consumers' income it may be of interest to express personal saving in terms of its purchasing power over consumers' goods and services since the purchase of such goods is the use of disposable income alternative to saving. In an analysis of capital transactions on the other hand it may be more relevant to express saving in terms of its purchasing power over the components of asset formation.

2. DIFFERENT ASPECTS OF THE PROBLEM OF INDEX-NUMBERS

In the extensive literature on price and quantity index-numbers different writers have approached the subject from widely different points of view. These viewpoints are encountered if an attempt is made to clarify and make precise the pragmatic statement of the problem given in the preceding section.

For the purpose of an introductory discussion it is convenient to concentrate on the case of a closed economy in which all production arising from foreign trade, government activity and asset formation is excluded. The basic commodity total of such an economy is the total unduplicated product which is equal to total final product or product absorbed by consumers. It is in respect of this total in the first place that measures of price and quantity movements are required.

A conceptual framework for this type of comparison is provided by economic theory. From this point of view a comparison may be attempted from the consumers' or from the producers' standpoint. The questions of whether consumption or production are higher in the current period than in the base period and if so by how much can be made more precise by means of the usual apparatus of indifference curves and production isoquants. These theoretical developments are useful as a guide to the nature of the comparisons sought but from a practical point of view they do not provide the basis for a solution since even in highly simplified cases much too little is known about preferences and production possibilities. If the comparisons made are required to provide unequivocal indications of changes in welfare or productiveness then it is useless to attempt them because the necessary empirical information is not available.

If this point of view is accepted then it becomes necessary to define the basis of comparison in pragmatic terms which can be given an operational significance. The basis adopted in this Report is the familiar one of constructing weighted arithmetic averages of price ratios and of quantity ratios, the weights being the expenditures on the different commodities in one of the two periods to be compared. A base-period (period 0) quantity index is obtained by taking the sum of the current-period (period 1) quantities each multiplied by its base-period price and by dividing this number by the total expenditure in the base period. A quantity index constructed in this way measures the proportionate increase in expenditure in the current over the base period which would have taken place if the quantities in each period had been as they actually were while the prices in each period had been equal to the prices in the base period.

In a similar way a base-period price index is obtained by taking the sum of the current-period prices each multiplied by its base-period quantity and by dividing this number by the total expenditure in the base period. A price index constructed in this way measures the proportionate increase in expenditure in the current over the base period which would have taken place if the prices in each period had been as they actually were while the quantities in each period had been equal to the quantities in the base period.

For many purposes it is convenient to establish measures in absolute rather than relative terms. This is particularly so in the case of the measurement of quantity movements. Thus, for example, it may be useful to express the level of total output or of total final expenditure for a series of years in terms of the system of relative values which held

12

in one of those years. Since these totals are made up of constituent outputs and final purchases it would be a desirable feature of the absolute measures that they should be additive. This property is in fact possessed by the measures suggested in the preceding paragraphs. Further, as will be clear from Chapter III, the measure proposed for total output at base-year prices is in principle identical to the measure of total final purchases valued according to the same system of relative values. As a consequence it is possible to draw up a balancing account in real terms which shows the industrial sources and final uses of total domestic production.

This account is the analogue in real terms of the familiar consolidated production account which shows in money terms the sources and uses of total domestic product. If the index-number system is so defined that, for any commodity total, the price index multiplied by the quantity index equals the value index then the relevant price index-numbers provide the links between the entries in the real and money accounts. As is well-known this equality holds for the type of index-numbers considered in this Report but not in a unique manner. This question is further considered in section 5 of Chapter III.

Apart from these properties which are useful from the point of view of consistency, the simple measures described above also have the advantages that their nature can be explained in simple terms and that they are relatively easy to calculate.

The construction of averages of price and quantity ratios presupposes that commodities are classified and provided with appropriate units in terms of which their quantity can be measured. If the usual pragmatic basis for index-numbers just outlined is accepted then it is these questions of classification and the establishment of units which form the central practical problem of putting index-numbers on a satisfactory operational footing.

The main practical difficulty arises because commodities and their varieties are exceedingly numerous and constantly changing. If a very detailed specification of commodities were adopted it would usually be found that many of the specifications were not available in the two periods to be compared so that direct comparison would be impossible. If on the other hand a broad specification of commodities were adopted, the categories in the commodity classification would not be homogeneous and there would be a danger that comparisons based on such a classification would be distorted.

In constructing a quantity index, the constituent quantities are valued by reference to their prices in the base period. If two different varieties of a commodity sell at different prices in the base period it is to be inferred that they are in some relevant sense different. The solution of the present problems involves the explanation of base-period price differences in terms of various measurable characteristics of the commodity. This is an empirical matter. If a relationship between price and quality characteristics can be found then different varieties can be reduced to comparable terms. In these terms the problem of new models and

13

new products is seen in its proper light namely as a difficulty which arises when changes are so large that they cannot with any certainty be fitted into the base-period system of relative values.

Quality differences in the ordinary sense of the term are only one out of a number of influences which result in price differences within commodity groups. Other factors which contribute to this result are the location of producers and consumers and the nature of the retail outlets in which goods are bought and sold. These differences lead to differences in base-period prices for apparently similar commodities which ought not to be ignored.

Another important source of price variation arises from seasonal changes in demand and supply. If comparisons are only made between years and if each season's supply is treated as a distinct commodity no difficulty arises. But difficulties do arise if this seasonal detail is not available or if comparisons are required between different seasons. In this situation an attempt must be made to reduce seasonal varieties to quantity units which are comparable in terms of their base-period values. This can be done by adjusting quantities with respect to the normal seasonal pattern of prices in the base year. With these units interseasonal comparisons can also be made.

The various difficulties just indicated call for a considerable amount of empirical knowledge about the variation of prices and the demand and supply factors which influence them. The object of the procedures outlined above is to make it possible to reduce the difficulties associated with the heterogeneity of commodities; they cannot, of course, help to dispel the basic ignorance regarding preference fields and production possibilities.

The objective so far has been to obtain a consistent system of price and quantity measures for commodity flows. This system in fact constitutes the set of index-numbers available. The adjustment of non-commodity flows to terms of constant prices is considered in relation to this system. It is shown that the kind of consistency that can in principle be attained for commodity flows cannot be attained in the case of non-commodity flows.

3. THE ARRANGEMENT OF THE REPORT

The arrangement of this Report is as follows. In Chapter II the economic theory of index-numbers is briefly discussed mainly in order to bring out the basic difficulties that are encountered in any attempt to apply this theory. From a practical point of view it is virtually impossible to measure or even order commodity totals by reference to a common characteristic such as utility. Instead it is necessary to concentrate on the more modest tasks of measuring actual price and quantity movements and of combining these to provide measures of central tendency for different parts of the economy or for the economy as a whole.

Chapter III is largely devoted to providing a conceptual framework for a consistent system of index-numbers for commodity flows. This framework involves an extension of the *Standardised System* to include a detailed statement of commodity flows between industries. As was noted in the preceding section, the establishment of a consistent system of index-numbers provides in the first place a balancing account in real terms of the sources and uses of domestic production in all its forms and in the second place the links between the entries in this account and its counterpart in money terms.

Chapters IV, V and VI are concerned with various problems arising from the heterogeneity of commodities. Chapter IV is devoted mainly to the problem of quality differences and changes and suggests a means, based on the relationship of prices to quality characteristics, whereby the difficulties encountered under this head might in practice be reduced. Chapter V is devoted mainly to heterogeneity due to locational factors and to the way in which this is likely to show itself on different plans for arranging the basic data on commodity flows. Chapter VI contains a discussion of the treatment of seasonal commodities and provides a scheme for carrying out seasonal adjustments of varying degrees of complexity.

Chapter VII is concerned with the treatment of non-commodity flows and the difficulties encountered in attempting to extend a consistent system of index-numbers into this field.

Chapter VIII contains a discussion of a number of problems of measurement such as the question of the selection of indicators and the choice of a base-period. Chapter IX contains a brief comparison of familiar types of index-numbers with the system presented here. A summary of the main conclusions which seem to emerge from the Report is given in Chapter X.

II

INDEX-NUMBERS AND ECONOMIC THEORY

1. INDEX-NUMBERS FROM THE CONSUMER'S POINT OF VIEW

The lessons to be drawn from the economic theory of index-numbers and its limitations can be seen by considering a simple type of economy in which all final product is devoted to personal consumption. In this situation the index-number problem may be set out as follows. Between two periods the consumption (or final product) of some commodities has risen while that of others has fallen per head of the population. Quantity and price measures for each commodity are available for each period and the total population in each period is known. In these circumstances what can be said about the real change in total consumption, or final product, per head and about the associated price level?

Suppose, in the first place, that there is only one consumer. If this consumer's preference field (or utility function) were known and if all the commodities consumed in both periods were represented in it then the problem would admit of a solution in terms of the theory. For by inserting the quantities of the different commodities consumed into the utility function the utility level attained in each period, 0 and 1, could be ascertained. If only an ordinal preference field can be established the solution will take the form: situation 1 is better than (or worse than or equivalent to) situation 0. If a cardinal preference field can be established a numerical measure of the difference between the two situations can be given.

The same knowledge on the part of the investigator would also enable a price comparison to be made since this problem could be stated in the form: what is the minimum amount of money that the consumer must be given in period 1 if he is to be able to achieve the same level of utility that he attained from his expenditure in period 0? Given the preference field, the purchases of period 0 and the price structure of period 1 this sum of money can be discovered. The change in the price level is then the sum in question divided by the expenditure of period 0.

This brief account based on the theory of consumers' behaviour provides a clear statement of objective. From a practical point of view,

17

however, the theory has severe limitations. In the first place actual comparisons involve difficulties not present in the above example and in the second place the necessary information about preference fields does not exist.

Complications of the first type arise as follows. First, even if there is only one consumer it is always possible that his tastes may change. If such a change takes place between the periods to be compared the comparison will depend on whether the base-period or the current-period system of preferences is used as the basis for the comparison. Second, even if the consumer's attitude to needs, wants and desires remains in some basic sense unchanged the invention of new commodities and the cessation of production of old ones may render any comparison difficult because the available commodities at the two dates cannot be directly compared. This is the problem of quality changes and new products which can only be handled satisfactorily if commodities can be fully described in terms of underlying characteristics each of which can be valued at the dates to be compared.

A third complication arises because in practice comparisons are usually required not in relation to an individual but in relation to a community: in the present case in relation to consumers as a whole. This being so it is clear that even if a perfect comparison could be made for each individual there would remain the problem of combining individual experiences to provide a comparison for consumers as a whole.

It might be argued that the comparison would be acceptable if made by reference to the average consumer assumed to have a well-defined preference field in terms of which preferences with respect to the commodities actually available in both periods could be expressed. Even if this basis were accepted the second type of limitation referred to above would come into operation since it would still be necessary to estimate the parameters of a preference field: in this case the one assumed to apply to the average consumer. This is an empirical task the formidable nature of which can easily be understood. It would be necessary to formulate various plausible expressions for the preference field, derive from them relationships (in practice demand equations) which could be examined empirically, observe the ability of these demand systems to relate actual experience, choose among them and estimate the parameters in the system chosen.

In the following section a specific example is given which indicates the kind of information that would be required if an attempt were made to make use of the welfare approach to index-number construction. In the present state of knowledge such information is not available and so it cannot serve as a basis for the construction of index-numbers. The ideas which have been outlined are useful for the following reasons. First, they give content to such concepts as real consumption which might otherwise be vague and obscure; second, they bring out the fundamental difficulties in establishing empirical correlates to concepts such as real consumption and so help to show what can and what cannot usefully be attempted in the present state of knowledge; finally they show the circumstances in which particular empirical correlates, such as a measure of real consumption which can actually be constructed, are likely to provide a good or a bad approximation to the concepts of the theory. This last point may be developed as follows.

If the individual consumer is in equilibrium, that is to say if he is maximising the satisfaction he can obtain from spending his income given the price situation, then his purchase of each commodity in his budget will be pushed to the point at which its marginal utility is proportional to its price, the factor of proportionality being the same for all commodities. Thus prices provide a system of relative values which is relevant to the individual in the neighbourhood of his equilibrium consumption pattern. If relative prices did not change there would be no index-number problem for the individual. The price level would change by the common ratio of current to base-period prices and quantity levels could be ordered by reference to the ratio of expenditure to the price level in different periods. If relative prices do change no such definite statements can be made without a knowledge of the preference field.

In the case of many consumers each one may be assumed to be adjusted in the base period to the base-period system of relative prices. If relative prices remain constant a comparison could therefore be made for each consumer. But the weight to be attached to each consumer would still depend on the possibility of inter-personel comparisons of utility.

In all these comparisons it is assumed that the purchases of each period relate to the same set of commodities or commodity characteristics. If this is not the case certain purchases would have to be left out of the comparison.

2. AN EXAMPLE : THE LINEAR EXPENDITURE SYSTEM

The kind of difficulties just described can be illustrated by an example in which a plausible approximation to an expression for a preference field is associated with a system of demand equations which might in practice be handled statistically. Suppose that for the *ith* commodity, $i = 1, \ldots, n$, the average individual's expenditure function is of the form

$$p_i q_i = b_i \mu + \sum_j (\delta_{ij} - b_i) c_j p_j \qquad (2.1)$$

In this expression p_i and q_i denote respectively the price of commodity i and the quantity of it which is bought while $\mu = \sum_i p_i q_i$ denotes the average individual's total expenditure. The b's and c's form a set of $2n-1$ independent parameters which characterise the average individual's demand system being restricted by the fact that $\sum_i b_i = 1$. The symbol

19

δ_{ij} is unity if $i = j$ and otherwise zero. The whole set of expenditure equations of the form (2.1) can be expressed by the matrix equation

$$\hat{p}\,q = b\,\mu + (I - bi')\,\hat{c}\,p \tag{2.2}$$

where μ has the same meaning as before, p and q denote respectively the price vector and the quantity vector, i and I denote respectively the unit vector and the unit matrix and b and c denote respectively vectors with elements b_i and c_i. Vectors are to be understood as column vectors and a row vector is expressed as the transpose of a column vector and denoted by a prime superscript. Diagonal matrices are denoted by the corresponding vector surmounted by a circumflex accent: for example $\hat{p}i = p$.

In the system (2.2) the expenditures on individual commodities as given by their respective functions sum identically to total expenditure, the quantities are homogeneous functions of μ and p so that there is no money illusion and the Slutsky condition (that the matrix of elasticities of substitution be symmetric) is satisfied. These are generally considered to be desirable properties of a demand system. In this case also the Marshallian demand curves are hyperbolae and the Engel curves, for given p, are straight lines with slopes b_i/p_i. However, the system essentially characterises a world of substitutes from which inferior and complementary goods are absent. The kind of behaviour which it describes can be seen most clearly by rewriting (2.2) in the form

$$\hat{p}\,q = \hat{p}\,c + b\,(\mu - p'\,c) \tag{2.3}$$

In this expression the vector c may be interpreted as a set of basic quantities to which the individual feels himself committed and his first act is to buy this set of quantities at the cost of $p'c$. The amount left to be spent $(\mu - p'c)$, which may be termed supernumerary income and which would be negative if committed expenditure, $p'c$, were greater than income, μ, is then devoted to the different goods in proportions given by the elements of b. The behaviour characterised by the system may thus reflect a considerable amount of inertia (if the c_i are relatively large) and this also seems a reasonable feature of the system.

With all its limitations this system has at least the merit that it can be applied and one method of doing this has been set out by Stone [22]. As has been shown by Samuelson [17] and by Geary [11] the preference field (or utility function), v say, associated with (2.2) is given by

$$log\ v = b'\ [log\ (q - c)] \tag{2.4}$$

or any monotonic transformation of this expression. Thus if b and c were known the value of v could be calculated for any given q. The finding $v_1 > v_0$ would indicate that the utility level of period 1 was greater than the utility level of period 0 but the question by how much it was greater would not in this case be uniquely defined.

20

It is also the case, as has been shown by Klein and Rubin [14], that if consumers' behaviour can be expressed by the system (2.2) then it is possible to construct a unique measure of the change in the cost of living between two dates. The cost of living may be defined by reference to a given base period as the minimum amount of money which the consumer needs so that with the price structure of the current period he can attain the level of utility which he actually attained in the base period. This amount of money, μ_1 say, is given by the expression

$$\mu_1 = p'_1 c + [(\mu_0 - p'_0 c)\, \gamma_1 / \gamma_0] \tag{2.5}$$

in which the subscripts 0 and 1 refer respectively to the base and the current period and γ_t denotes a weighted geometric average of the prices of period t with the elements of b as the weights. The cost of living in the current period is thus given in terms of the base-period level by the ratio μ_1/μ_0.

3. INDEX-NUMBERS FROM THE PRODUCER'S POINT OF VIEW

It can be seen from the last section that index-number comparisons cannot in general be interpreted as welfare comparisons unless individual preference fields are known and comparable. Consideration will now be given to the possibility that such comparisons can be interpreted in terms of productiveness.

Given a set of final products (consumers' goods and services in this example), there can be imagined a large number of lists showing in quantity terms the mixtures of these products which could be produced with given technology and resources. These lists correspond to points in commodity space and these points may be supposed to be enclosed by a surface which represents the production possibilities of the system for given technology and resources. If production possibilities are being maximised so that the productive system is in a sense efficient then the quantitative list of commodities actually produced will correspond to a point on the surface. Precisely which point will depend on the tastes of consumers and the extent to which each is able to realise his desires. If tastes or the distribution of incomes change a competitive productive system will tend towards a new equilibrium point on the surface. To each point there will correspond a set of relative prices.

In these terms a production comparison could be attempted on the following lines. Given a list of final products, larger or smaller lists of the same composition could be obtained by multiplying each quantity in the list by a common factor greater or smaller than unity. The current-period list could be said to represent an increase of production compared with the base period if in the base period only a smaller list of current-period composition could be produced. A quantitative measure of the change would be given by the common factor of proportionality. This line of thought has been developed by Debreu [6].

21

This would seem a simpler and more direct approach than the one described in the preceding section and so, perhaps, it is. But again it involves empirical knowledge, namely estimates of the parameters of the base-period production possibility surface. It can also be seen that there is no reason to expect the same numerical answer if the role of base and current periods are interchanged.

4. PRACTICAL POSSIBILITIES

Thus attempts to construct price and quantity comparisons which can be interpreted unequivocally in terms of welfare or productiveness founder on a lack of empirical information. For this reason it is not possible to measure indifference levels for consumers or their analogue for producers, though on certain simplifying assumptions it may appear that some collections of commodities are inferior to a given collection while others, but not all others, are superior to it. It is, however, possible to measure the average price and quantity changes for collections of commodities in terms of a given system of relative values and in practice the construction of price and quantity index-numbers amounts to doing just this.

Throughout this Report, index-numbers are discussed in operational terms. They are regarded simply as measures of the average change in prices or in quantities over a particular period defined in a particular way. No claim is made that they necessarily indicate, still less measure, changes in welfare or productiveness or in the price movements associated with these concepts. The reasons for this cautious attitude towards concepts from which index-numbers are frequently supposed to derive their interest and importance have already been given but several further points must now be clarified if the position adopted in this Report is not to be misunderstood.

First, it would be wrong to conclude that index-numbers are without use or interest because they cannot meet certain theoretical requirements. Consider, for example, quantity index-numbers of consumers' expenditure. These provide a measure, based on the relative prices ruling in the base period, of the average change in the intake of commodities by consumers between the base and the current period. Such information is essential to any summary appraisal of economic change and to the tracing of economic regularities on a manageable scale. A list of the hundreds, or even thousands, of constituent changes would be hard to assimilate without an estimate of their central tendency which is what an index-number provides.

Second, to continue with the same example, if an index-number of consumers' expenditure is carefully constructed it should provide a good estimate of this central tendency in terms of the base-period system of relative values. What it cannot do, for the reasons already given, is to allow for the changes in utility which accompany changes in the collection of commodities bought by consumers. An interpretation of the changes

22

in terms of welfare does not therefore emerge directly from the calculations but it is often possible to form some impression of this aspect of the matter by observing the composition of the change in consumption in the light of what is known from the analysis of family budgets about the division of commodities into luxuries, necessaries, inferior goods, etc.

Thus over a period in which production and consumption have on the whole been rising per head of the population it may be found that the principal exceptions to this general tendency are a certain group of commodities which are known from other evidence, for example household budget studies, to be inferior goods, that is to say goods which tend to be bought in larger quantities by poor households than they are by rich households. If this fact is known the uncertainty about whether, on the average, consumers have become better off or worse off, induced by the fact that while the consumption of some commodities has risen the consumption of other commodities has fallen, is diminished; indeed the fact that it is the consumption of inferior goods that has fallen tends to reinforce the belief in improvement gained from observing the rise in the consumption of other commodities. In a similar way it may also be possible to discover, from information outside the observations from which the index-number was constructed, what has been happening to the distribution of incomes and in this way it may be possible to rebut the hypothesis that the apparent improvement in average consumption has mainly been concentrated in a limited section of the community.

Third, it must not be supposed, from the practical difficulties encountered in applying the economic theory of index-numbers, that the measures described in this Report have a purely technical connotation from which all economic considerations are absent. It will be abundantly clear in what follows that economic considerations are involved at almost every stage of the argument and that one of the main conceptual problems from a practical point of view consists in so defining the terms in which quantities are measured that it is possible to express what is available at two dates in terms of the system of relative values existing at one of them.

Thus index-numbers, like other averages, should be regarded as a means of reducing large quantities of data to manageable proportions. On their own limited ground of a fixed system of relative values they are capable of providing relatively accurate measures. It is important to keep in mind their limitations which arise largely from a lack of empirical knowledge and it is useless to ignore them altogether on the ground that the information they can provide is not, from a certain point of view, ideal.

An example of the usefulness and limitations of index-numbers arises in connection with the part played by retail price indices in wage negotiations and wages policy. Such index-numbers are frequently constructed by using base period expenditures to weight the price ratios of the constituent commodities. In this case an individual with fixed tastes and circumstances whose base-period consumption pattern is the same as in the index and whose income is adjusted in proportion to it would retain his base-period utility level if all prices moved in the same proportion. But if relative prices changed he could, if his income were regulated as above, improve his utility level in the current period by making adjustments in his consumption pattern. In this context it is important to know the average change in prices but many other factors have also to be taken into consideration.

5. THE VALUATION OF COMMODITIES

In common with the procedures usually adopted in price and quantity comparisons, the index-numbers considered in this Report have the form of weighted averages of price or quantity ratios. In fact they are the weighted arithmetic and harmonic averages associated with the names of Laspeyres and Paasche. Their characteristics and their relationship to one another in a social accounting framework are described in the following chapter. The weights used in making the averages are the base- or current-period values of the component transactions. Assuming for the moment that quantity measures which form the subject of Chapter IV, are available, there remains the question of commodity valuation.

Available price information takes the form of market prices and this basis of valuation could be applied throughout the index-number calculations. From the point of view of consumers it would seem to be the most suitable since relative market prices are the best available approximation to relative marginal utilities in the base period. From the point of view of producers on the other hand it would be better to adopt a system which approximated to base-period marginal costs.

In a fully adjusted perfectly competitive system with no impediments to production or consumption, marginal cost and marginal utility ratios would both be given by the ratios of market prices. In practice impediments of various kinds may exist which prevent the above equalities from being maintained. In such circumstances price ratios do not possess the convenient interpretation that has so far been placed on them.

On the side of production, producers in various industries operate under conditions which are removed, to a greater or less extent, from perfect competition. In conditions of imperfect competition and monopoly, prices will tend to be above marginal costs but the extent to which this is so will vary in different industries. So far as this element in the situation is concerned market prices could only usefully be abandoned if marginal costs were known, and this information, in the overwhelming majority of cases, is not available.

There is, however, a second feature on the production side for which allowance can be made. If indirect taxes and subsidies are present, and especially if their relationship to price is very different for different commodities, it seems reasonable to think that, in valuing different output changes, unit costs should be restricted to that part which is composed, directly or indirectly, of the remuneration of the factors of production and so approximates the essential cost of producing the various commodities. This can be done if the market price of each

24

commodity is adjusted by the subtraction of accumulated indirect taxes and the addition of accumulated subsidies per unit of that commodity. The implications of this operation are set out in section 7 of Chapter III below.

While this basis of valuation has much to commend it in the case of output index-numbers it is not equally appropriate to the construction of index-numbers of consumption and other constituents of final product. It will be evident, however, that if a consistent system of index-numbers is to be constructed then a single basis of valuation must be chosen. For, if this is not done, alternative sets of weights will be applied to a given set of indicators with the consequence that the resulting index-numbers, must, in general, show some discrepancy. In practice this discrepancy may be small at least so far as quantity index-numbers for the main aggregates are concerned, but, except in over-simplified cases, it will not be possible to find an analytical expression which connects the alternative systems of index-numbers.

It is sometimes suggested that in the construction of production index-numbers a modification of the above treatment should be adopted. According to this line of thought an industry's output should be valued at market prices less the indirect taxes actually paid by the industry while an industry's inputs should be valued at market prices since these are the prices which are relevant to purchasing decisions. The weight attached to each industry's net output at constant values is the same as in the factor cost calculation but the indicators of net output will, in general, be different. A set of such production index-numbers will not average out to an index of final product since intermediate product is valued higher as an input than as an output and so will not cancel out.

The decomposition of market prices into accumulated factor costs and accumulated indirect taxes implies, in the general case, a knowledge of technological structure. In special circumstances, or if simplifying assumptions can plausibly be made, it is possible to carry out the calculations even where this knowledge is lacking. Thus in the case of production index-numbers it can easily be seen that if inputs could in all circumstances be assumed to be proportional to outputs then the quantity indicator for any industry's gross output would equal the quantity indicator for its input and therefore also the quantity indicator for its net output. In such a case the quantity movement of each industry's net output could be represented by a single indicator, as in practice it very frequently is, and if these indicators are weighted by the appropriate totals of direct factor costs an aggregate index-number on a factor cost basis of valuation will be obtained. Again if indirect taxation is, in every industry, the same constant proportion of net output it follows that in each industry accumulated factor costs are proportional to price so that the same quantity index is obtained on either basis of valuation.

In the case of final expenditure index-numbers it can frequently be assumed that the greater part of indirect taxation and subsidies are levied on final product and do not re-enter the productive system as part of the

25

cost of intermediate output. If it can further be assumed that the remaining indirect taxes and subsidies are everywhere the same proportion of net output then the accumulated factor costs per unit for final products can be obtained by first deducting the known specific indirect taxes (less subsidies) per unit from the corresponding final product prices and by then deducting the balance of indirect taxes (less subsidies) from the adjusted totals of final product values on a pro rata basis.

On the side of consumption the principal institutional feature which may prevent the adjustment of purchases to the point at which the ratio of price to marginal utility is equal for every commodity in the consumer's budget is a system of commodity rationing. If such a system is in force many consumers will have to forego further purchases of rationed commodities while the marginal utility to them of these commodities is still relatively high. This state of affairs would present no special difficulties if preference fields were known. In the absence of this knowledge an attempt may be made to assess by means of demand analysis the changes in the price structure that would have to come about in order that the collection of commodities actually bought under rationing should be bought under free market conditions. These changes would show that the free market prices of rationed commodities would be high in relation to their actual prices and that the opposite tended to hold true for unrationed commodities. Consequently if quantity ratios of rationed purchases to previous free market purchases were weighted by previous purchases at the calculated prices, relatively large weights would be given to commodities the consumption of which might be expected to have fallen more or risen less than the average for all commodities. Many difficulties would be met in attempting to apply such a method as this. For example the virtual prices, as they have been termed by Rothbarth [16], needed to make purchases under rationing acceptable under free market conditions, would, in general, be different for different consumers; for those unaffected by rationing no change would be involved. On this whole subject reference should be made to Tobin's survey of the theory of rationing [23] and to the papers cited there.

The essential feature of rationing from the present point of view is that it limits the extent to which consumers can adjust their purchases so as to maximise utility. It is not relevant merely that it changes the pattern of consumption. Such changes are taking place all the time for a variety of reasons but this fact does not call for any special adjustment.

The conclusion of this section is that ideally it would be desirable to carry out the calculations on both a market price and a factor cost basis of valuation. Unless various simplifying assumptions are adopted, as in practice is the case, the former basis will be the easier to use. Factor cost calculations, however, are of particular interest in setting out the industrial composition of value added at constant prices. If, as will certainly be desirable where possible, the calculations are carried out both by industry of origin and by final product it is essential to adopt the same basis of valuation in each case if the numerical consistency of the two methods is to be checked.

26

III

INDEX-NUMBERS IN A SOCIAL ACCOUNTING FRAMEWORK

1. THE PRODUCTION BOUNDARY

This Report is concerned with the adjustment of all kinds of flows appearing in the national accounts to terms of constant prices. A crucial step to this end is the construction of consistent price and quantity index numbers for commodity transactions which are here defined as transactions in goods and services other than factor services.

Any attempt to make more precise the meaning attached to the term commodity flow may conveniently start with a discussion of what is to be included and what excluded. A productive system may be regarded as a system of transformation processes in which natural resources, other factors of production and products are combined to produce other products. These transformation processes take place in establishments and may conveniently be grouped together into industries. The first problem to examine is the points at which the transformation processes are deemed to begin and end. In this way a boundary can be set to the concept of production which is relevant for the present purpose.

In the case, for example, of agriculture, capital is used to buy equipment and to finance current expenses pending the sale of the product and is combined with natural resources, labour and goods and services such as artificial fertilisers, petrol and the professional maintenance of mechanical equipment to produce agricultural output. The contribution of agriculture to the total value of production is less than the total value of output from agriculture since a part of the latter is matched by inputs from other industries such as chemicals, petroleum refining and service garages. The contribution of agriculture must therefore be defined in terms of the value added by agricultural activity to these inputs from other industries. This in turn requires that the term industry be limited since if all the inputs into agriculture were deemed to be supplied by industries then the concept of value added in agriculture would disappear and this would equally be true with regard to every other industry. This emptying out of the concept of value added is avoided by distinguishing between the provision of services by the factors of production and other inputs. The former are not deemed to be provided by industries whereas the latter are. Thus, for example, there are no industries which ultimately supply labour or capital though there may be industries which organise and direct this supply.

This notion of ultimate inputs whose remuneration (including positive or negative residual profits if the transformation processes are not in equilibrium) constitutes value added in each transformation process (or industry) is generally accepted and forms the basis of the measurement of the total value of product and its distribution among industries. Its significance lies in the fact that it is the total value of remuneration which accrues in one way or another to the human agents in the system.

It is equally important to consider the ultimate output of the productive system. In one sense the treatment of ultimate outputs has already been decided since they may be equated to the outputs of the transformation processes which are absorbed by the factors of production. In a closed system the value of these outputs must exactly equal the value of the remuneration of the factors of production; for all remaining output flows will cancel out since they will appear as the output of one transformation process and the input into another. This fact may be re-stated in the propositions that all product is either intermediate product or final product and that final product in a closed economy is identically equal in value to the remuneration of the factors of production or to the total of value added in all the transformation processes.

From another point of view, however, these matters are not so readily settled. The measurement of ultimate inputs in quantity as opposed to value terms lies outside the scope of this Report and will not be considered further. The measurement of ultimate outputs, however, still presents a problem. Suppose, for the sake of simplicity, that the whole of the remuneration of the factors of production accrues directly to households, the value of whose services constitutes the sole ultimate component of cost. The value of final product is the value of the goods and services which households buy from industries. It may be assumed that a quantity, as opposed to value, measure can be assigned to each element of final product and that a measure of the total quantity change between two or more periods can be formed by valuing the constituent quantities of final product at the prices paid in a base period. It may then be said that this measure is inadequate because in fact further transformation takes place in the households and that this ought to be taken into account. Is it sufficient to measure final product by reference to the input into households or is it desirable to go further and attempt to measure the input of the different products (prepared meals rather than ingredients) into the members of the household? This question can be posed differently by asking where the boundary should be drawn between human activity which forms part of production and that which forms part of other aspects of life.

The view taken in this Report is that productive activity should be deemed to stop at inputs into households and that no attempt should be made to search for ultimate forms of production beyond this point.

28

If the usual national accounting convention of not imputing a value to household activities is adopted, as it is here and in the *Standardised System*, then the above results would seem to follow fairly clearly. For if there is no value added in households then any attempt to construct a quantity index for the net output of households will result in a series the elements of which are indeterminate. This might be regarded as a sufficient objection. On the other hand it might be argued that, in measuring production, an attempt ought to be made to impute a value to household activity and also to seek indicators of household outputs as well as of household inputs. The objection to such a course is the difficulty, if not impossibility, of following it. The essential difficulty lies in the construction of quantity measures of household output which have any independent validity. It is clear that the housewife and other members of the household transform household purchases before they are finally consumed but it is not clear that a useful quantity measure can be assigned to the results of their activity. Thus, for example, one of the transformation processes carried out in households is the conversion of food raw materials and other ancillary commodities into prepared meals. How could a useful quantity measure be assigned to the output of prepared meals?

It seems evident that the number of meals, even the number of meals of different kinds, would not provide a useful measure since the quality of the meals might be changing. Indeed such a measure would be inferior to a quantity indicator of food and other inputs which is the measure recommended here. It might be possible, however, to adjust this indicator by reference to the amount of work in preparation but in such a case it would be necessary to give the indicator of work done a positive weight, that is it would be necessary to impute a value added in households in respect of the preparation of meals. If such a course were adopted it might still be doubted whether anything of substance had been gained since the essential element of skill in the preparation of meals would almost certainly elude any measure of work done so that the proposed adjustment would contain little, if any, relevant information and it would be better to avoid a pretence of measuring something which in fact is not amenable to measurement.

It may be objected that so far as this example is concerned households are in exactly the same position as restaurants which supply meals and that presumably restaurants are to be regarded as engaged in productive activity. This is a perfectly valid point but it tells rather against the possibility of obtaining a good output indicator for restaurant services than in favour of extending such uncertainties to the much larger constituent, households. In fact, in constructing an indicator for restaurant output it would be necessary to take account of inputs, foods, fuel, etc., from other industries. In addition it would be possible to take account of labour input and to weight the resultant indicator of output by the total selling value of restaurant output in the base period. In this case it would be more reasonable to ignore market imperfections and to assume that more labour contributed to more restaurant service than would be the case with households. Moreover the value added and the changing amount of labour involved can in fact be measured. It must be recognised however that such a built-up indicator of output is far from ideal and there seems little case for extending such methods voluntarily into areas where the components are not readily measurable.

It is probable that most experienced investigators would agree that little purpose is to be served in the present context by attempting to carry the idea of productive activity into households. There is of course the question of paid domestic service but this is usually handled by including an item of labour input along with the other purchases by households. In the case of government activity however the arguments for stopping short at the inputs into the final buyer are often considered less cogent.

The problem is illustrated by the example of public education. Thus it may be asked: does the public education system have an output distinct from the weighted sum of its inputs, it being recognised that direct labour input is an important element? It can always be said that there is something called education which those engaged in teaching produce with the aid of books, pens and paper but it is quite another thing to propose a quantitative indicator of the amount of education which is not built up from the inputs into the educational system. Obvious examples such as the number of pupils educated even if weighted in some way by the educational tests that they pass seem, on inspection, to be inferior to a measure of educational output based on weighted inputs including labour inputs.

The conclusions of this section may now be summarised. No attempt is made in this Report to propose quantity measures for the ultimate inputs into the productive system; that is the inputs of the factors of production. Ultimate outputs on the other hand are measured by the outputs reaching final buyers and among these is included direct labour absorbed by final buyers. Such labour inputs may be thought of as emanating from service activities and as providing a measure of the quantity of the output of these activities. These proposals are made in the light of existing experience in the measurement of inputs and outputs. They incorporate a limited concept of productivity and may be superseded by the development of objective measures of various forms of human activity. It may be claimed however that in the present context it is more useful to confine measures of input and output within the boundaries here proposed than to extend these boundaries into what, for the present at any rate, seems a largely arbitrary field.

2. AN EXTENSION OF THE STANDARDISED SYSTEM

If the argument of the preceding section is accepted then the production boundary implicit in the *Standardised System* can be accepted for the present purpose and it is only necessary to extend the accounts described there by the introduction of separate production (operating) accounts for each industry. The resulting accounting structure and its relevance in the construction of index-numbers can best be indicated by a numerical example such as is set out in table 1 overleaf.

TABLE 1. A NUMERICAL EXAMPLE OF A TRANSACTIONS MATRIX

		PRODUCTION ACCOUNTS						OTHER ACCOUNTS			TOTAL
		AGRI-CULTURE	MINING	MANU-FAC-TURING	UTIL-ITIES	CON-STRUC-TION	OTHER INDUS-TRIES	EXTER-NAL	CAPITAL TRANS-ACTIONS	APPRO-PRIA-TION	
Production Accounts	Agriculture	0	0	608	0	0	1	9	4	459	1,081
	Mining	6	0	208	127	27	56	48	—9	103	566
	Manufacturing	299	85	0	72	372	490	2,063	737	3,902	8,020
	Utilities..........	4	9	132	0	8	88	4	39	258	542
	Construction	30	21	57	2	0	121	2	637	375	1,245
	Other industries ...	105	30	860	65	80	0	499	56	6,223	7,918
Other Accounts	External	53	11	1,475	1	39	1,098	0	437	44	3,158
	Capital transactions ...	50	25	320	50	20	250	165	0	1,021	1,901
	Appropriation Factor incomes ...	578	382	3,579	202	692	4,999	368	0	0	10,800
	Indirect taxes (net) ...	—44	3	781	23	7	815	0	0	0	1,585
Total	....	1,081	566	8,020	542	1,245	7,918	3,158	1,901	12,385	36,812

In this presentation each row and column pair relate to an account, the outgoings, by convention, being placed in the columns and the incomings being placed in the rows. The accounts are all in consolidated form and so the total of recorded transactions which appears in the bottom right-hand corner of the table is of no particular significance. There are nine accounts in the system; six are production accounts for the six industries among which productive activity is divided, one is an appropriation account, one a capital transactions account and one an external account or account for the rest of the world.

The incomings of the six production accounts are obtained in the main from sales of goods and services as shown in the first six rows of the table. The only exception lies in the fact that the value of the net physical increase in stocks is included along with sales of fixed assets in the column relating to capital transactions. This arrangement follows the treatment usually adopted but it would always be possible as an alternative to regard drafts on stocks as a cost item in production and to include them in the row relating to capital transactions. The outgoings of the six production accounts, which appear in the first six columns, of the table, comprise: (i) purchases from other production accounts, (ii) imports, (iii) provisions for depreciation and (iv) net value added which in turn is distributed between (iva) outgoings to the factors of production and (ivb) indirect taxes less subsidies.

The entries in the non-production accounts can also be described very simply. Thus the external account row shows the incomings accruing to the rest of the world from: (i) the sale of commodities which are imports into country which is being studied, (ii) borrowing from that country and (iii) current transfers (net) from that country. The outgoings in the external account column comprise: (i) the purchase of commodities which are the exports of the country being studied, (ii) capital transfers (net) to that country and (iii) factor income payments (net) to that country. The netting of the entries for foreign transfers and factor income payments and their precise arrangement in the table are, of course, arbitrary but the treatment adopted was chosen so that the incomings in the first row of the appropriation account should sum to the national income [1] and that all incomings into the appropriation account should sum to the net national product at market prices.

The incomings of the capital transactions account comprise: (i) provisions for depreciation made by each of the industries, (ii) capital transfers (net) from abroad and (iii) saving in the country under investigation. The corresponding outgoings relate either to gross domestic asset formation or to lending abroad (net) and in total comprise the country's gross addition to wealth.

The remaining account is the consolidated appropriation account of the country which is being studied and all the entries in it have already implicitly been described. The incomings of this account take the form

---

1. The table is based on the estimates for the United Kingdom in 1950 given in [4].

32

of (i) factor income payments received either from the productive activity of the country or from abroad (net) the sum of which is the national income and (ii) the indirect taxes less subsidies payable (or receivable) by the different industries. The outgoings comprise (i) final current expenditures on goods and services by private consumers and general government, (ii) current transfers (net) abroad and (iii) saving.

3. COMMODITY FLOWS IN THE PRODUCTION ACCOUNTS

The first question which will be considered in relation to table 1 is the derivation of the gross domestic product at market prices which amounts to 12,732. This total can be reached as the sum of at least four economically interesting sets of transactions.

First, it is possible to calculate the contribution of each industry to the gross domestic product at market prices. This may be done by taking for each industry the excess of the value of the commodities sold over that of the commodities bought, as set out in the following table.

	VALUE OF COMMODITIES SOLD [1]	VALUE OF COMMODITIES BOUGHT	CONTRIBUTION TO GROSS DOMESTIC PRODUCT AT MARKET PRICES
Agriculture	1,081	497	584
Mining	566	156	410
Manufacturing	8,020	3,340	4,680
Utilities	542	267	275
Construction	1,245	526	719
Other industries	7,918	1,854	6,064
All industries	19,372	6,640	12,732

[1] Including the value of the physical increase in stocks.

Second, it is possible to calculate the final expenditure on the products of the economy, that is to say the sum of current and capital expenditures at home on commodities and the net value of commodities exported. This calculation may be set out as follows:

	PURCHASES FROM OR SALES (—) TO						
	AGRI-CUL-TURE	MIN-ING	MANU-FAC-TURING	UTIL-ITIES	CON-STRUC-TION	OTHER INDUS-TRIES	ALL INDUS-TRIES
Current expenditure on goods and services	459	103	3,902	258	375	6,223	11,320
Gross domestic asset formation	4	—9	737	39	637	56	1,464
Exports	9	48	2,063	4	2	499	2,625
Less Imports..............	—53	—11	—1,475	—1	—39	—1,098	—2,677
Total	419	131	5,227	300	975	5,680	12,732

The composition of final expenditure in this example is shown in the final column of this table.

Third, the gross domestic product at market prices has just been obtained by first summing the elements in the first four rows of the above table and by then summing the column of these totals. Equally, however, it could be reached by first summing the elements in the first six columns and by then summing the row of these totals. The elements in this final row represent the net sales of each industry outside the productive system as a whole.

It is obvious that the last two ways of reaching the gross domestic product at market prices involve the summation of the same set of transactions. It is also true, as may at once be verified, that the set of transactions which are summed to give the gross domestic product at market prices by the first method is identical with that involved in the other two methods. For the first method is based on the net total of commodity sales for each industry and this means that all the inter- (and intra-) -industry commodity sales cancel out and leave a total which is composed of the net commodity sales out of the productive system as a whole.

This result leads to a proposition of fundamental importance in the construction of consistent systems of index-numbers relating to commodity transactions which may be stated as follows.

Given a system of commodity transactions, a basis of valuation (for example market prices or factor costs), a common base period and a set of quantity (or price) indicators which show the change from the base to another period of the quantity (or price) involved in each commodity transaction from one account to another, then the weighted average of these indicators reached by any of the three methods described above will yield an identical value for the real product (or the price level associated with it).

Thus in principle an index of the aggregate real value added in a productive system (an index of production) is identical to an index of net sales out of the productive system as a whole which may be regarded as composed either of the net sales of each industry out of the productive system as a whole or of current and capital final expenditures adjusted for imports and exports (an index of final expenditure). If in practice these alternative measures are found to diverge this can only be due to imperfections of data or to inconsistencies of treatment. The relationship between net output index-numbers (the first method) and final product index-numbers (the second method) is set out algebraically in section 6 of this chapter.

There is in fact yet a fourth way of building up an aggregate equal in value to the gross domestic product at market prices from the elements of table 1. This is done by adding together all outlays by the industries of the country under investigation in respect of factor services, net indirect taxes and provisions for depreciation. It is not obvious that any meaning could be attached to the association of price and quantity components with these transactions and for the moment this question

34

will not be discussed. Even if such an association were possible, however, it is clear that the elements in the total would in every case be different transactions from those which appeared in each of the first three summations. Accordingly there is no reason to suppose that the quantity and price changes of total product arrived at by this route would, even if they existed, be the same as those arrived at by the other three routes. This conclusion is not surprising since, if net indirect taxes and depreciation provisions are neglected, this route leads to a measure not of real output but of real (factor) input. These two measures would necessarily diverge if there were any net change in the productivity of the factors.

4. GROSS AND NET CONCEPTS

In the derivations of total product given in the last section provisions for depreciation are not treated as commodity flows and value added is defined before these provisions are deducted. As a consequence domestic product and asset formation appear on a gross and not on a net basis.

In the *Standardised System* the term depreciation provision covers that element of cost which relates to the wearing out of fixed assets used in current production. No attempt will be made here to describe the numerous problems which are encountered in obtaining a quantity indicator of this element of cost but it may be useful to give an indication, based on simplifying assumptions, of the kind of measure that is involved.

Consider a durable commodity, say a particular kind of machine, and let q denote the quantity of this commodity bought in the current period either by the community as a whole or by a particular industry. This quantity is in part a net addition to the opening stock of the commodity and in part a replacement of that part of the stock which is used up in the current period. Thus

$$q = v + u \qquad (3.1)$$

where v denotes the net investment in the commodity in the current period and u denotes the depreciation of the existing stock. If depreciation is measured by a reducing balance formula with a fixed depreciation rate of $1/(m + 1)$, the depreciation in the period on the opening stock of s, say, is $s/(m + 1)$ while the depreciation in the period on the purchases of the period will, in general, be a somewhat smaller proportion of these purchases since they are not all concentrated at the beginning of the period. If this proportion is $1/(km + 1)$, then the depreciation of the period is

$$u = s/(m + 1) + q/(km + 1) \qquad (3.2)$$

In this equation $m \geqslant 0$ and $k \geqslant 1$. If, independently of m, $k = 1$, then it is implied that the purchases of the period are concentrated at its outset. If, on the other hand, the more realistic assumption is made that

35

purchases are spread evenly through the period then k is related to m by the relationship

$$k = 1 / [m\{(m+1) \log_e [(m+1)/m] - 1\}] \qquad (3.3)$$

The larger is m, the more durable is the commodity under consideration and, as $m \to \infty$, $km \to \infty$ and $k \to 1$. Conversely, the smaller is m, the more perishable is the commodity and, as $m \to 0$, $km \to 0$ and $k \to \infty$.

If E^θ denotes an operator which retards the variable to which it is applied by θ time units so that $E^\theta q\,(t) \equiv q\,(t+\theta)$, then the closing stock of the commodity may be denoted by Es. This closing stock is equal to the opening stock plus the net investment of the period. That is

$$Es = s + v \qquad (3.4)$$

If v is added to both sides of (3.2) there results, from (3.4),

$$q = Es - \frac{m}{m+1}s + \frac{1}{km+1}q$$

$$= \frac{km+1}{km}Es - \frac{km+1}{k\,(m+1)}s \qquad (3.5)$$

so that

$$s = \frac{km}{km+1}E^{-1}q + \frac{m}{m+1}E^{-1}s$$

$$= \frac{km}{km+1}\sum_{\theta=1}^{\infty}\left(\frac{m}{m+1}\right)^{\theta-1}E^{-\theta}q$$

$$= \frac{k\,(m+1)}{km+1}\sum_{\theta=1}^{\infty}\left(\frac{m}{m+1}\right)^{\theta}E^{-\theta}q \qquad (3.6)$$

from which it can be seen that as $m \to 0$, $s \to 0$ and as $m \to \infty$, $s \to \sum_{\theta=1}^{\infty}E^{-\theta}q$. Finally

$$u = \frac{1}{km+1}q + \frac{k}{km+1}\sum_{\theta=1}^{\infty}\left(\frac{m}{m+1}\right)^{\theta}E^{-\theta}q \qquad (3.7)$$

Thus, from (3.7), a series for u, the depreciation of the period can be built up from a knowledge of past purchases, $E^{-\theta}q$, the durability factor, m, and the assumption that purchases are spread evenly through the period. This is a reasonable assumption since, by hypothesis, the period chosen is the shortest period for which data on purchases are available. The series for u is in the same units as the series for q and so can be converted to base-period values by multiplication by the price of the commodity in the base period.

As already emphasized, the foregoing is no more than an indication of the means by which depreciation at constant prices might be measured. The reducing balance formula may not be considered a good approximation to the way in which durable goods actually wear out even if they are operated in a normal manner for an indefinite period. It might be desired to allow for variations in the amount of use per period and also for the retirement of the durable good after a finite life time. Problems connected with changes in technology or demand and the question of provision for damage are not considered at all. All these questions will be deferred for the time being.

5. THE CHARACTERISTICS OF AGGREGATIVE INDEX-NUMBERS

Aggregative index-numbers of prices and quantities are widely used by economic statisticians and in the usual symbolism of index-numbers may be set out as follows:

	FOR PRICES	FOR QUANTITIES
Base-weighted (Laspeyres' formula)	$\dfrac{\Sigma p_1 q_0}{\Sigma p_0 q_0} \equiv \Lambda$	$\dfrac{\Sigma p_0 q_1}{\Sigma p_0 q_0} \equiv L$
Current-weighted (Paasche's formula) ...	$\dfrac{\Sigma p_1 q_1}{\Sigma p_0 q_1} \equiv \Pi$	$\dfrac{\Sigma p_1 q_1}{\Sigma p_1 q_0} \equiv P$

This notation is elliptical but has long been used and will be adopted here. The symbol $\Sigma p_1 q_0$ is used to denote $\sum_i p_{1i} q_{0i}$ where i relates to the ith of the n commodities of the system. The subscripts 0 and 1 relate respectively to the base period and to the current period which is to be compared with it. Thus $\Sigma p_1 q_0$ denotes the sum of the values obtained by adding up the quantities of the base period each multiplied by its price in the current period, that is the vector product of base-period quantities and current-period prices. Thus, for example, the base-weighted aggregative for quantities is obtained by revaluing the quantities of the different commodities bought (or sold) in the current period (period 1) at the prices ruling in the base period (period 0) and by dividing the resulting value by the value of purchases (or sales) in the base period.

All the index-numbers have the form of the ratio of value sums. It can easily be seen however that, for example,

$$\Sigma p_0 \, q_1 / \Sigma p_0 \, q_0 = \Sigma \, [p_0 \, q_0 \, (q_1 / q_0)] / \Sigma \, p_0 \, q_0 \qquad (3.8)$$

Thus the base-weighted quantity index is a weighted arithmetic average of the n quantity ratios (q_{1i}/q_{0i}), the weights being the base-period expenditures $(p_{0i} \, q_{0i})$. In a similar way it can easily be seen that the current-weighted quantity index is a weighted harmonic average of the n quantity ratios (q_{1i}/q_{0i}), the weights being the current-period expenditures $(p_{1i} \, q_{1i})$. Thus with index-numbers of the Paasche type the weights change as successive periods are compared with a given base period. Precisely similar relationships hold in the case of price index-numbers.

The index-numbers have the following convenient properties. The relative change in the actual value of the commodity transactions considered may be written as $\Sigma p_1 \, q_1 / \Sigma \, p_0 q_0 = V$ say. It can then be seen that

$$\Sigma p_1 \, q_1 / \Sigma \, p_0 \, q_0 \equiv (\Sigma \, p_1 \, q_1 / \Sigma \, p_0 \, q_1)(\Sigma \, p_0 \, q_1 / \Sigma p_0 \, q_0) \qquad (3.9)$$

$$\equiv (\Sigma \, p_1 \, q_0 / \Sigma \, p_0 \, q_0) \, (\, \Sigma p_1 \, q_1 / \Sigma \, p_1 \, q_0) \qquad (3.10)$$

or, more briefly,

$$V \equiv \Pi \, L \qquad (3.11)$$

$$\equiv \Lambda \, P \qquad (3.12)$$

so that the product of a current-weighted price index and a base-weighted quantity index or of a base-weighted price index and a current-weighted quantity index yields identically the change in value of the aggregate of transactions. Thus the relationship relative change in price times relative change in quantity equals relative change in value holds for the appropriate pairs of these index-numbers as it does for individual commodities but it is always possible to establish the identity in two ways. If unique measures of price and quantity changes are required which satisfy this condition the easiest way to obtain them is to take the geometric means of the two price index-numbers and of the two quantity index-numbers since, as can be seen from (3.11) and (3.12)

$$\sqrt{\Pi \, \Lambda} \ \sqrt{L \, P} \ \equiv V \qquad (3.13)$$

The measures of price and quantity changes given in (3.13) have the form of the " ideal " index-numbers proposed by Irving Fisher [9]. It has been shown by Siegel [18] that this index-number system can be generalised to cover cases in which more than two multiplicative factors (for example quality as well as price and quantity) contribute to a product having a unique index expression. The form proposed by Fisher and the more complicated forms proposed by Divisia [7] may be useful for

38

the technical purpose of removing small discrepancies between L and P or between Λ and Π but where both the base- and current- weighted index-numbers can be calculated it is desirable that they should be given separately. For the valuations appropriate to each situation may be so different that the comparison is dominated by the set of valuations which is adopted as the basis of comparison. This fact will emerge if the two index-numbers are given separately but it will be hidden if they are averaged. Unless a means is found of justifying a particular form of averaging such as the " ideal " formula in economic terms it must, if it is to be used, be justified as a helpful convention which can be regarded as legitimate because the discrepancy to be removed is in some sense small.

There is a further useful property of aggregative index-numbers which arises from the fact that component value sums can always be added to give their total. Thus, for example,

$$\Sigma p_0 q_1 / \Sigma p_0 q_0 \equiv \Sigma [p_0 q_0 (p_0 q_1 / p_0 q_0)] / \Sigma p_0 q_0 \qquad (3.14)$$

It can be seen from the numerator of this expression that values expressed in constant prices can be obtained by adding together component values similarly expressed. As the example shows the base-weighted quantity index is identically equal to the weighted arithmetic average of similar expressions for its components. Index-numbers of this form can therefore be weighted (by base-period weights) and averaged to yield the similar index for the aggregate of transactions to which they relate. Similar relationships hold in the case of current-weighted aggregative index-numbers.

Finally it should be remembered that $\Pi > \Lambda$ and $P > L$ if there is a positive correlation between the price and quantity relatives while $\Pi < \Lambda$ and $P < L$ if the correlation is negative. In the ordinary case of falling demand curves and rising supply curves, positive correlation is to be expected where the changes between the two dates to be compared are dominated by changes on the side of demand which bring about shifts in the demand curves. In a similar way negative correlation is to be expected where supply changes are dominant.

6. THE APPLICATION OF THE INDEX-NUMBERS TO A SYSTEM OF COMMODITY FLOWS

It has already been shown in section 3 above that the domestic product can be reached by aggregating commodity transactions in various ways and that this fact gives rise to three different methods of expressing the domestic product in constant prices which, in principle, are identical. The relationships involved have been set out by Stone and Hansen [19] and by Stone and Prais [20]. An alternative, and perhaps simpler formulation may be given as follows.

If all non-commodity transactions including provisions for depreciation are excluded from it, table 1 appears as follows:

TABLE 2. A COMMODITY FLOW MATRIX BASED ON TABLE 1

		PRODUCTION ACCOUNTS						OTHER ACCOUNTS			TOTAL
		AGRI-CULTURE	MINING	MANU-FAC-TURING	UTIL-ITIES	CON-STRUC-TION	OTHER INDUS-TRIES	EXTER-NAL	CAPITAL TRANS-ACTIONS	APPRO-PRIA-TION	
Production Accounts	Agriculture	0	0	608	0	0	1	9	4	459	1,081
	Mining	6	0	208	127	27	56	48	—9	103	566
	Manufacturing	299	85	0	72	372	490	2,063	737	3,902	8,020
	Utilities	4	9	132	0	8	88	4	39	258	542
	Construction	30	21	57	2	0	121	2	637	375	1,245
	Other industries	105	30	860	65	80	0	499	56	6,223	7,918
Other Accounts	External	53	11	1,475	1	39	1,098	0	*	*	2,677
	Capital transactions	*	*	*	*	*	*	*	0	*	*
	Appropriation	*	*	*	*	*	*	*	0	0	*
	Total	497	156	3,340	267	526	1,854	2,625	1,464	11,320	22,049

NOTE. Asterisks denote zero entries arising from the removal of non-commodity transactions from table 1.

40

This accounting system for commodity flows and its constituent transactions can be represented by the partitioned matrix T^* where

$$T^* \equiv \begin{bmatrix} W & X & a \\ Y & Z & b \\ h' & g' & \sigma \end{bmatrix} \qquad (3.15)$$

in which the partitions correspond to the thick lines in table 2. Thus if, in general, there are m production accounts and $(n-m)$ non-production accounts the matrix is of order $(n+1)$ and the elements in the various partitions have the following connotations:

W denotes an $m \times m$ matrix of purchases by production accounts from production accounts, that is of intermediate products.

X denotes an $m \times (n-m)$ matrix of purchases by other accounts from production accounts, that is of final expenditures at home and exports.

Y denotes an $(n-m) \times m$ matrix of purchases by production accounts from other accounts, that is of imports.

Z denotes an $(n-m) \times (n-m)$ matrix of purchases by other accounts from other accounts. In the present example it contains only zero elements. If, however, final expenditures abroad had not, for convenience, been routed through one of the production accounts. these would have appeared as elements of Z.

a denotes a (column) vector 'of m elements. Its typical element, a_r say, represents the total incomings into production account r from commodity transactions, that is sales and any net increase in stocks.

b denotes a (column) vector of $(n-m)$ elements. Its typical element, b_s say, represents the total incomings into other account s from commodity transactions. In the present case every element of b is zero except the one which relates to the external account and this represents the total value of imports.

h' denotes a (row) vector of m elements. Its typical element, h'_r say, represents the total outgoings from production account r in respect of commodity purchases, that is to say the total value of intermediate products including imports absorbed by industry r.

g' denotes a row vector of $(n-m)$ elements. Its typical element, g'_s say, represents the total outgoings of the sth other account in respect of commodity purchases, that is to say the total value of final product absorbed by other account s.

σ denotes a scalar, the total value of commodity transactions recorded in the matrix. Thus $\sigma = i'_n \begin{bmatrix} a \\ b \end{bmatrix} = [h' \ g'] i_n$ where i_n denotes a unit (column) vector of length n and i'_n denotes its transpose, namely a unit (row) vector with n elements each equal to unity.

41

Let w_{ij}, x_{ij}, y_{ij} or z_{ij} denote the element of W, X, Y or Z respectively which stands in the ith row and jth column of T^*.

For production account r the contribution to total product is given by either of the two equivalent expressions

$$\left(\sum_{j=1}^{m} w_{rj} + \sum_{j=m+1}^{n} x_{rj} \right) - \left(\sum_{i=1}^{m} w_{ir} + \sum_{i=m+1}^{n} y_{ir} \right) = a_r - h', \quad (3.16)$$

If this expression is summed over all production accounts there results the total domestic product which can be written as

$$\sum_r \left[\left(\sum_{j=1}^{m} w_{rj} + \sum_{j=m+1}^{n} x_{rj} \right) - \left(\sum_{i=1}^{m} w_{ir} + \sum_{i=m+1}^{n} y_{ir} \right) \right]$$

$$= i'_m [WX] i_n - i'_n \left[\begin{matrix} W \\ Y \end{matrix} \right] i_m$$

$$= i'_m a - h' i_m$$

$$= i'_m (a - h) \quad (3.17)$$

The sums in (3.17) can also be written as

$$\sum_r \left(\sum_{j=m+1}^{n} x_{rj} - \sum_{i=m+1}^{n} y_{ir} \right) = i'_m (X - Y') i_{n-m} \quad (3.18)$$

since

$$\sum_r \left(\sum_{j=1}^{m} w_{rj} - \sum_{i=1}^{m} w_{ir} \right) = i'_m W i_m - i'_m W' i_m = 0 \quad (3.19)$$

Similarly the contribution of non-production account s to total final expenditure is given by

$$\left(\sum_{i=1}^{m} x_{is} + \sum_{i=m+1}^{n} z_{is} \right) - \left(\sum_{j=1}^{m} y_{sj} + \sum_{j=m+1}^{n} z_{sj} \right) = g'_s - b_s \quad (3.20)$$

If this expression is summed over all non-production accounts there results the total final expenditure which can be written as

$$\sum_s \left[\left(\sum_{i=1}^{m} x_{is} + \sum_{i=m+1}^{n} z_{is} \right) - \left(\sum_{j=1}^{m} y_{sj} + \sum_{j=m+1}^{n} z_{sj} \right) \right]$$

$$= i'_n \left[\begin{matrix} X \\ Z \end{matrix} \right] i_{n-m} - i'_{n-m} [YZ] i_n$$

$$= g' i_{n-m} - i'_{n-m} b$$

$$= i'_{n-m} (g - b) \quad (3.21)$$

The sums in (3.21) can also be written as

$$\sum_s \left(\sum_{i=1}^m x_{is} - \sum_{j=1}^m y_{sj} \right) = i'_{n-m} (X'-Y) i_m \qquad (3.22)$$

since

$$\sum_s \left(\sum_{i=m+1}^n z_{is} - \sum_{j=m+1}^n z_{sj} \right) = i'_{n-m} Z' i_{n-m} - i'_{n-m} Z i_{n-m} = 0 \quad (3.23)$$

It is obvious that the sums in (3.18) and (3.22), and therefore in (3.17) and (3.21), are identical being, in fact, alternative ways of expressing the sum of the elements of X minus the sum of the elements of Y.

The elements of the sub-matrices, W, X, Y and Z of the commodity flow matrix, T^*, represent the quantities of a given period each multiplied by its respective price. All the above propositions would hold however if these elements represented the quantities of one period each multiplied by its respective price in another period. If the suffixes 0, 1 are attached to the elements of T^* to denote the prices of period 0 multiplied by the quantities in period 1 and so forth, then the various index-numbers for the economy as a whole may readily be set out. The Laspeyres and Paasche quantity index-numbers, denoted by L and P, are given by

$$L = i'_m (X_{01} - Y'_{01}) i_{n-m} / i'_m (X_{00} - Y'_{00}) i_{n-m} \qquad (3.24)$$

and

$$P = i'_m (X_{11} - Y'_{11}) i_{n-m} / i'_m (X_{10} - Y'_{10}) i_{n-m} \qquad (3.25)$$

while the corresponding price index-numbers, denoted by Λ and Π, are given by

$$\Lambda = i'_m (X_{10} - Y'_{10}) i_{n-m} / i'_m (X_{00} - Y'_{00}) i_{n-m} \qquad (3.26)$$

and

$$\Pi = i'_m (X_{11} - Y'_{11}) i_{n-m} / i'_m (X_{01} - Y'_{01}) i_{n-m} \qquad (3.27)$$

The constituent index-numbers for the different industries, the different final buyers and the different commodity components, of final expenditure, can be set out in various ways as suggested in [20] which can be derived from the treatment given above. In writing down the expressions for the index-numbers relating to the different industries it is necessary to reintroduce the elements of W since intermediate product cancels out for the economy as a whole but not for separate industries.

It can thus be seen that the aggregation of quantity indices of net output yields a figure which is identical to that obtained by aggregating quantity indices of final expenditure since in the former approach everything which is not final expenditure cancels out. The net output calculation may be useful for two reasons. First, it shows the net contribution of each productive sector to total domestic product. Second, the available data may make it possible to carry out a more reliable calculation on this basis than could be obtained by an attempt to adjust the components of final expenditure for changes in prices.

7. MARKET PRICES AND FACTOR COSTS

Now that the form of the index-numbers and the framework into which they fit have been described, it is possible to discuss the relationships between systems of index-numbers constructed on alternative bases of valuation as indicated in section 4 of Chapter II.

It is convenient to consider the simple case in which technological conditions are assumed to be such that in each industry each input is proportional to output. All output forms part either of intermediate or final product and so the distribution of product between these two classes is given by

$$q = Aq + e \tag{3.28}$$

where q denotes a vector of industry outputs, e denotes a vector of final demands and A denotes a matrix of input-output coefficients. In a similar way an equation for the formation of prices is given by

$$p = A'p + f + t \tag{3.29}$$

where p denotes a vector of prices, f denotes a vector of factor costs per unit of output incurred in each industry, t denotes a vector of indirect taxes (less subsidies) per unit of output payable by each industry and A' is the transpose of A. In (3.29) the price per unit of the output of the *ith* industry is shown as composed of three types of element, namely: (i) the *ith* element of $A'p$ that is the total cost of the inputs from other industries per unit of output of industry i; (ii) the factor costs incurred in industry i per unit of its output; and (iii) the indirect taxes (less subsidies) payable by industry i per unit of its output. It can also be seen from the same equation that

$$p = (I - A')^{-1}f + (I - A')^{-1}t \tag{3.30}$$

where the first term on the right-hand side of the equation represents accumulated factor costs and the second term represents accumulated indirect taxes.

In the system just described the construction of index-numbers of production is, in principle, as simple as the construction of index-numbers of final product since the fact that, *ex hypothesi*, inputs are in all cases proportional to outputs means that the quantity indicator of an industry's output can be applied to its value added in the base period without any explicit consideration of inputs.

In the notation used here the value of final product is the vector product $p'e$. In this expression no indication is given of the periods to

44

which p and e relate but for example p'_0e_1 might be used to denote the sum of current-period final products each multiplied by its price in the base period. The relationships which follow can be interpreted as relating to quantities of one period multiplied by unit values (market prices, factor costs, net indirect taxes as the case may be) of another.

The numerators and denominators of production index-numbers which sum to final product are readily derived as follows. From (3.29)

$$p' = (f' + t') (I - A)^{-1} \qquad (3.31)$$

and, from (3.28)

$$e = (I - A) q \qquad (3.32)$$

whence

$$p'e = (f' + t') q \qquad (3.33)$$

which expresses the equality of final expenditure on domestic product and domestic product itself on a market price basis of valuation. Since, from (3.28),

$$t'q = t'(I - A)^{-1}e \qquad (3.34)$$

it follows that (3.33) can be rearranged to give

$$[p' - t' (I - A)^{-1}] e = f' q \qquad (3.35)$$

which expresses the equality of final expenditure on domestic product and domestic product itself on a factor cost basis of valuation. It can readily be seen that even in the simple case assumed the weights to be attached to the quantity indicators in (3.33) and (3.35) are, in general, different whence index-numbers constructed on the two bases will also be different. The exception to this statement occurs if net indirect taxes levied on an industry are, in every industry, the same proportion of value added. In this case the elements of t are proportional to the elements of f and the two bases yield the same index-numbers.

In section 4 of Chapter II a modified form of production index-number on a factor cost basis was mentioned in which, in the present notation, outputs are weighted by the elements of $p - t$ and inputs by the elements of p. In the simple case considered here the numerators and denominators of the production index-numbers would reduce to $f'q$ as in (3.35) but the final product index-numbers would be given by $(p' - t')\ e$. Since from (3.28)

$$t'q = t'Aq + t'e \qquad (3.36)$$

it follows that (3.34) can be rearranged to give

$$(p' - t')\ e = (f' + t'A)\ q \qquad (3.37)$$

which illustrates the fact that this system which involves different bases for the valuation of inputs and outputs cannot, in general, be self-consistent.

45

IV

COMMODITIES, QUANTITY UNITS AND QUALITY DIFFERENCES

1. THE OBJECTS OF COMMODITY TRANSACTIONS

The construction of a system of price and quantity index-numbers was seen, in the preceding chapter, to involve tracing the flow of commodities, that is goods and services other than the services of the factors of production, between all the transactors (or sectors) in the economy. A means must then be found of expressing each commodity flow in terms of appropriate quantity units. The associated price measure will also depend on the quantity unit chosen.

Many commodities are complicated and can only be adequately specified in terms of a number of characteristics. The specification of commodities, as has been amply illustrated by Brems [1], can be drawn up either in consumers' or producers' terms. It is desirable to find a specification which is common to buyers and sellers so that each commodity flow which is an input from the buyer's point of view and an output from the seller's point of view shall be given a unique formulation and unit of measurement. It is proposed in this Report that in attempting to measure inputs and outputs guidance should be sought in the first place from the understanding of buyers and sellers as to the nature of the objects that pass between them.

This may seem a self-evident proposal and at the same time one which is almost devoid of practical implications. Such, however, is not the case. Consider the example of a wheat farmer whose product consists solely of a certain standard grade of wheat into which the possibility of quality variation does not enter. Stock variations may also be ignored for the present purpose and it may be assumed that in each period the whole of the crop is sold. The total output (= volume of sales) in each period can be suitably measured by weight but its amount, even on the assumption of constant acreage sown and constant inputs from other industries, will vary with climatic conditions. In these circumstances the gross output of the wheat farmer will vary in quantity terms with the weight of his crop and the net output will vary as the difference between the weight of the crop valued at base-period selling value and a quantity measure of inputs from other industries weighted by their base-period cost to the farmer. Thus net output will depend on the amount of wheat produced in relation to inputs from other industries. The effort put out by the farmer and other conditions of the productive process are irrelevant except insofar as they lead to a change in the quantity of wheat produced or to a change in inputs from other industries.

In a similar way the particular situation of consumers is implicitly left out of account. In measuring the final output of coal going to consumers it is sufficient to attend to the quantity and, as far as possible, grade of coal that goes to the consumer and no attention need be paid to the further questions of how and in what circumstances the consumer uses it. These questions would depend on the characteristics of consumer's coal-burning equipment, on climatic conditions and on many other considerations. Such factors are undoubtedly relevant to the utility or satisfaction which the consumer obtains from the coal he buys just as climatic conditions are clearly relevant to the disutility that the wheat farmer suffers from the production of his crop. They are not, however, relevant to the quantity measures of consumption and production with which this Report is concerned and these, accordingly, are limited in content by the proposal made in this section.

The conclusions drawn so far will probably command fairly general assent and could of course have been stated as guiding principles in their own right and not as implications of a more general principle. The proposal made has, however, other implications.

Thus, for example, it can be applied to ascertaining the appropriate unit of quantity in passenger transport. Under one system of charging the passenger buys the right to make a journey of unspecified length on the transport system. In such a case the appropriate quantity unit for the output of the transport system is the journey. An alternative system of charging requires that the passenger buys the right to travel a certain distance, the fare being proportional to this distance. In this case the appropriate quantity unit is the passenger-mile. It will be seen that if the method of charging is changed a comparison of periods before and after the change would require in principle different quantity indicators depending on the period chosen as the basis for the comparison. An alternative justification of this treatment emerges from the analysis of section 2 below.

2. QUALITY VARIATIONS AND VARIETY CHANGES

It was implicitly assumed in the preceding section that the same commodities were available in the two periods to be compared and that they could be classified into homogeneous categories which could be specified in a manner acceptable to buyers and sellers as a description of the objects that passed between them. These assumptions taken together would imply a lack of variation in commodities which is far removed from the actual state of affairs. In practice most commodities

48

are produced in numerous varieties the precise specification of which is constantly changing. Thus an attempt to apply the proposal of the preceding section would seem to imply either a very coarse specification of commodities in which most of the quality variations would be lost or an immensely detailed classification of varieties which would also have serious disadvantages. In the first place it would hardly be possible to record commodity data in such detail and in the second place, if this were done, it would be found that there was little that could be directly compared in the outputs of two different periods.

What is required in this situation is to find some means of comparing varieties in terms of quality differences that command a price. This requirement can be met if it is possible to establish a relationship between price and quality characteristics in the base period, the quality characteristics being also those which are relevant in the current period. This method will now be described and illustrated and in terms of it a number of practical problems and procedures will be discussed.

As an example, consider the case of beer. It will be assumed that the main quality difference among varieties of beer lies in their alcoholic content or strength and that this factor alone need be taken into consideration. The strength of beer is capable of continuous variation but in practice only a limited number of varieties are produced. If certain particular varieties were always produced, the appropriate treatment, assuming sufficiently detailed information to be available, would be to regard each one as a separate commodity. Since however strengths tend to change from time to time in such a way that in two periods there might be no beers of exactly the same strength produced in both, it is clear that the above treatment would break down. What is required in such a case is some means of assessing the importance to be attached to strength in comparing the quantity or price of beer produced in two periods.

In the case of beer it is usually recognised that there are two measures of quantity, liquid volume and alcohol volume, represented respectively by bulk and standard barrels. The problem of adjusting for quality changes could in this case be expressed by asking in what way bulk and standard barrels should be averaged in order to give a true measure of quantity change on a base-period system of valuation.

This question can be answered if it is possible to establish a relationship in the base period between the prices of different varieties of beer and their qualities defined in terms of the ratios of their quantity measures. Any such relationship can only be based on observations but as far as possible it should be capable of interpretation as an equilibrium relationship and should not be dominated by some abnormal occurrence in a particular period. Thus it may be found that in the neighbourhood of the base period there is a well-defined and on the whole stable relationship between the prices of varieties and their quality characteristics but that in the base period itself this relationship is upset by some transient phenomenon such as a strike or exceptional weather conditions which have destroyed the supply of a particular ingredient which enters differentially into beers of different qualities. In such circumstances it

49

would be desirable to take account of the experience in periods close to the base period which were not subjected to exceptional influences or, better still, to base the analysis on average experience in which the exceptional features might reasonably be expected to cancel out.

In the following example this kind of complication will be ignored. Thus let

q_r = quantity of beer measured in terms of liquid volume;

q_s = quantity of beer measured in terms of alcohol volume;

λ = q_s/q_r = quality, that is strength, of the beer;

v = expenditure on beer;

p_r = price of beer per unit of liquid;

p_s = price of beer per unit of alcohol.

Suppose that a relationship can be found, for the base period, between p_r and λ. Let the relationship take the simple form

$$p_{r0} = \alpha_0 + \beta_0\lambda$$
$$= \alpha_0 + \beta_0 \ (q_{s0}/q_{r0}) \tag{4.1}$$

If (4.1) is multiplied by q_{r0} there results

$$p_{r0} \ q_{r0} = \alpha_0 \ q_{r0} + \beta_0 \ q_{s0} \tag{4.2}$$

Thus the base period expenditure on beer is expressed as a weighted sum of the two quantity measures q_r and q_s. If (4.1) provides a good relationship between price and quality in the base period then (4.2) shows how the two quantity indicators should be weighted in order to obtain a Laspeyres quantity index for beer in which quality, in the sense of strength, is taken into account. Since

$$p_{r0} \ q_{r0} \equiv p_{s0} \ q_{s0} \equiv v_0 \tag{4.3}$$

it follows that

$$p_{s0} = p_{r0} \ q_{r0}/q_{s0} \tag{4.4}$$

If (4.1) is multiplied by q_{r0}/q_{s0} there results

$$p_{s0} = \alpha_0/\lambda + \beta_0 \tag{4.5}$$

which, when multiplied by q_{s0}, yields

$$p_{s0} \ q_{s0} = \alpha_0 \ q_{r0} + \beta_0 \ q_{s0} \tag{4.6}$$

a result which could have been derived at once by combining (4.2) and (4.3). However, a comparison of (4.1) and (4.5) brings out the relationships between the alternative price measures and the measure of quality.

In this way beer has been divided into two characteristics, liquid volume and alcohol volume, and α_0 and β_0 may be interpreted as the prices of these characteristics in the base period. Indeed it may be said that beer, as such, has disappeared from the list of commodities and that it has been replaced by two new commodities, r and s. The fact that r and s are constructs and not physically separable does not conflict with the guiding principle that in defining commodities attention should be paid to the understandings of buyers and sellers. These understandings are obviously concerned to an important extent with the subject of quality and the present formulation only serves to give a means of expressing this fact which is capable of empirical analysis.

The Laspeyres quantity index for beer takes the form

$$L = \frac{\alpha_0 q_{r1} + \beta_0 q_{s1}}{\alpha_0 q_{r0} + \beta_0 q_{s0}} \tag{4.7}$$

which, on the interpretation of α_0 and β_0 just given, is a base-weighted aggregative of commodities r and s. In terms of (4.7) it is irrelevant that beers cease to be produced in the precise strengths available in the base period, though if the strengths of beer came to lie altogether outside the base-period range there would naturally be a doubt as to the correctness of applying (4.1) in the new situation.

Estimates of α_0 and β_0 together with information on the prices and quantities of r and s in the base and current periods make it possible to construct a Laspeyres quantity index and a Paasche price index. If the complementary index-numbers are required then it is necessary to estimate α_1 and β_1, that is the parameters in the relationship between price and quality in the current period. If the ratio α/β is the same in both periods then the Laspeyres and Paasche index-numbers will be identical.

It can be seen from (4.1) that if $\beta_0 > 0$ and $\alpha_0 = 0$ then total alcohol content is the appropriate measure of the quantity of beer and no separate weight need be given to liquid volume. In this case beer should be measured in standard barrels. Similarly if $\beta_0 = 0$ and $\alpha_0 > 0$ then bulk barrels are the appropriate measure. In the construction of official index numbers of retail prices it is sometimes assumed, in terms of the present formulation, that $\alpha_0 = \beta_0$ so that equal weights are assigned to the two measures of quantity. It is doubtful whether this can be regarded as a realistic solution since it seems almost certain that while β is positive α is negative, that is to say there is some minimum strength at which beer would cease to command a positive price. If this is actually the case then a positive weight should be given to total alcohol volume and a negative weight should be given to liquid volume.

The results just given may be compared with the basic formula derived by Hofsten in his study of *Price Indexes and Quality Changes* [12]. In the notation used here this formula for the component of a price index-number may be written

$$\Lambda = \Pi = \frac{p_{r1}}{p_{r0}} \cdot \frac{1}{g} \tag{4.8}$$

where g is the ratio of a unit of quantity adjusted for quality in the current and base periods respectively. In the case where $\beta > 0$ and $\alpha = 0$, the appropriate price ratio is

$$\frac{p_{s1}}{p_{s0}} = \frac{p_{r1}}{p_{r0}} \cdot \frac{\lambda_0}{\lambda_1}$$

$$= \frac{p_{r1}}{p_{r0}} \cdot \frac{1}{g} \qquad\qquad (4.9)$$

If $\alpha \neq 0$ then only Π can be obtained from a base-period price-quality relationship. It is given by

$$\Pi = \frac{p_{r1}}{\alpha_0 + \beta_0 \lambda_1}$$

$$= \frac{p_{r1}}{p_{r0}} \cdot \frac{1}{g} \qquad\qquad (4.10)$$

since g is given by

$$g = \frac{\alpha_0 + \beta_0 \lambda_1}{\alpha_0 + \beta_0 \lambda_0} \qquad\qquad (4.11)$$

If a current-period price- quality relationship is available, then

$$\Lambda = \frac{\alpha_1 + \beta_1 \lambda_0}{p_{r0}}$$

$$= \frac{p_{r1}}{p_{r0}} \cdot \frac{1}{g} \qquad\qquad (4.12)$$

since, in this case,

$$g = \frac{\alpha_1 + \beta_1 \lambda_1}{\alpha_1 + \beta_1 \lambda_0} \qquad\qquad (4.13)$$

It is always possible that the apparent need to give a negative weight to one of the quantity measures arises from a faulty analysis of the relationship between price and quality. Thus there is no need for this relationship to be linear as in (4.1). It might, for example, be better to approximate this relationship by the expression

$$p_{r0} = \alpha_0 + \beta_0 \lambda_0 + \gamma_0 \lambda^2_0 \qquad\qquad (4.14)$$

whence

$$p_{r0} q_{r0} = \alpha_0 q_{r0} + \beta_0 q_{s0} + \gamma_0 q^2_{s0}/q_{r0} \qquad\qquad (4.15)$$

In this case it would be necessary to construct a third quantity measure, q^2_s/q_r and to give it a weight, γ_0.

This method of analysing quality differences can readily be generalised to handle any number of quality characteristics. Thus if price is linearly dependent not on one but on $n–1$ quality measures the set of equations (4.1) and (4.5) is replaced by

$$p = \hat{q}^{-1} i \, \theta' \, q \qquad (4.16)$$

and the set composed of (4.2) and (4.6) is replaced by

$$\hat{p} \, q = i \, \theta' \, q \qquad (4.17)$$

In these expressions p, q and θ are vectors each containing n elements. The elements of q are the various measures of quantity while those of p are the corresponding measures of price. The elements of θ are the parameters in the relationship between price and quality. Thus for the beer example (4.16) could be written out in full as

$$
\begin{bmatrix} p_{ro} \\ p_{so} \end{bmatrix} = \begin{bmatrix} 1/q_{ro} & o \\ o & 1/q_{so} \end{bmatrix} \begin{bmatrix} 1 \\ 1 \end{bmatrix} [a_0 \ \beta_0] \begin{bmatrix} q_{ro} \\ q_{so} \end{bmatrix}
$$

$$
= \begin{bmatrix} a_0 & + \beta_0 \ (q_{so}/q_{ro}) \\ a_0 \ (q_{ro}/q_{so}) & + \beta_0 \end{bmatrix}
$$

$$
= \begin{bmatrix} a_0 & + \beta_0 \lambda \\ a_0/\lambda & + \beta_0 \end{bmatrix} \qquad (4.18)
$$

as in (4.1) and (4.5).

The method that has been described could in principle be applied to a wide range of commodities. In each case relationships would have to be established for different periods between the prices of different varieties and their quality characteristics. It must now be recognised that commodity classifications are conventional being composed, say, of classes, sub-classes and varieties within sub-classes. In these terms the beer example relates to the analysis of varieties, different types of beer, within a sub-class beer. The method could in principle be equally well applied to the analysis of sub-classes, say beer, wine and spirits, within a class alcoholic drinks. In doing this it would not be necessary to relate only commodities that are conventionally grouped together and it would in principle be possible to extend the analysis to the whole range of commodities.

3. AN EXAMPLE OF THE RELATIONSHIP OF PRICE TO QUALITY

The application indicated at the end of the preceding paragraph provides a good example of the method just described and also illustrates the position that arises when, in the price-quality relationships, qualities have to be combined in a multiplicative rather than an additive manner.

From the *Brewers' Almanack* [2] the following information relating to the prices and strengths of different varieties of alcoholic drink can be compiled.

TABLE 3. PRICE AND STRENGTH OF VARIOUS FORMS OF ALCOHOLIC DRINK ON SALE IN THE UNITED KINGDOM IN 1941

	PRICE IN PENCE PER PINT	STRENGTH IN PER-CENTAGE OF PROOF SPIRIT	LOG PRICE	LOG STRENGTH
Beer :				
Mild ale, draught	8	5.48	0.9031	0.7388
Special stout in bottle	14	9.42	1.1461	0.9741
Dublin stout in bottle	18	9.16	1.2553	0.9619
Wine :				
Genuine Port A (over counter)	80	35.60	1.9031	1.5515
Australian red wine	52	35.70	1.7160	1.5527
South African red wine (over counter) ...	46	37.30	1.6628	1.5717
British wine (over counter)	20	29.90	1.3010	1.4757
Whisky :				
Scotch 30 under proof (over counter)	216	70.00	2.3345	1.8451
Scotch 35 under proof (over counter)	192	65.00	2.2833	1.8129
Scotch 30 under proof (in bottle)	144	70.00	2.1584	1.8451
Cider :				
Draught (over counter) ....?.....	6	7.24	0.7782	0.8597
Bottled	7	8.15	0.8451	0.9112

This information, which is readily accessible, is presented for illustrative purposes and not as a definitive study of the influence of alcoholic strength on the price of different drinks. The last two columns of the table show the common logarithms of p_r, the price per unit of liquid volume, and λ, the measure of alcoholic strength. Inspection of the data shows that there is a well-marked positive linear relationship between $\log p_r$ and $\log \lambda$. If the parameters of this relationship are determined by the method of least squares from the model

$$\log p_r = \alpha + \beta \log \lambda + \varepsilon \qquad (4.19)$$

it is found that $a = -0.190$ and $b = 1.27$ where a and b are the estimators of α and β. The magnitude of the correlation coefficient between $\log p$ and $\log \lambda$ is 0.95 indicating a close but not perfect relationship between the two variables. Thus apart from relatively minor discrepancies

$$p_r = 0.65 \, \lambda^{1.27} \qquad (4.20)$$

which, on multiplication by q_r, yields

$$p_r q = 0.65 \, \lambda^{1.27} \, q_r$$
$$= 0.65 \, (q_s^{1.27} \, q_r^{-0.27}) \qquad (4.21)$$

54

Equation (4.21) shows that a quantity indicator which takes account of strength can be made by taking the weighted geometric average of q_s and q_r shown in round brackets. The weights depend on the observed relationship between price and strength in 1941. The coefficient 0.65 (= antilog a) expresses (in pence per unit) the base year price appropriate to the quantity indicator $(q_s^{1.27} q_r^{-0.27})$.

Several features emerge from this example. In the first place it can be seen that a reasonably satisfactorily indicator of the quantity of alcoholic drinks can be formed without reference to the specific drinks or their varieties simply by forming an appropriate weighted geometric average of two quantity indicators for alcoholic drinks as a whole; namely liquid volume, q_r, and alcohol volume, q_s. If, for some reason, a single simple indicator must be used, q_s would be more suitable than q_r.

In the second place reference to table 3 indicates the respects in which this simple analysis of the quality of alcoholic drinks is in fact an oversimplification. It can be seen that the observations for both beer and cider bear out, approximately, so far as the parameter β is concerned, the general relationship (4.20) found for all kinds of drink. Accordingly (4.20) indicates approximately the importance that should be attached to strength as an indicator of quality in measuring the quantity of each of these types of drink taken separately. Ideally of course it would be desirable to have a larger number of observations in each case but this point will not be pursued here. It can also be seen, however, that for given strength the price of cider is somewhat below the price of beer so that there is a further, small, relevant difference between them other than strength. A more refined analysis would seek to take account of this difference. The simplest way to do this in the present case would be to treat beer and cider as separate commodities each with a separate quality equation. These relationships would, so far as can be seen from the data presented, have approximately the same slope but the intercept (log price) for cider would be lower than that for beer.

In the third place the very limited number of observations bear out the well-known fact that while, on the whole, wine fits into the general picture of the relationship of price to strength there are evidently a number of other quality characteristics that influence price in this case. In a refined analysis it would be necessary to track these down but if wine is a small item in total consumption and if the proportions in which wines of different qualities are drunk do not change very much a neglect of this refinement cannot be of much importance.

4. OTHER APPLICATIONS AND A COMPARISON WITH OTHER METHODS

It seems probable that an immense amount of information must be reasonably accessible in business records which would enable the relationship of price to quality characteristics to be determined for a wide range of commodities. Such information might be useful in the first place in bringing to light the more important quality characteristics in various cases and, in the second, if the necessary alternative quantity measures were available or could be obtained, in improving the accuracy of price and quantity index-numbers. The appropriateness of the method and its possible range of application can be seen from a discussion of a number of examples.

In the first case it can at once be applied to confirm the conclusion reached in section 1 of this chapter about the treatment of alternative methods of charging for passenger transport. Let it be supposed that the journeys provided by the transport service differ only by a single quality characteristic, their length, λ. Assume further, as in section 1, that the price per journey, p_r, is a linear function of λ, that is, as in (4.1)

$$p_r = \alpha + \beta\lambda \qquad (4.22)$$

In the case of the constant charge per journey $\beta = 0$ and so the appropriate quantity indicator is q_r, the number of passenger journeys since q_s, the number of passenger miles, obtains a weight of zero. On the other hand if the charge is proportional to distance $\alpha = 0$ and the appropriate quantity indicator is q_s. In practice it is quite likely that both α and β will be positive since there is a cost associated with distance travelled and a further cost associated with stopping the vehicle to let the passenger get on and off, issuing and checking his ticket, etc. which is independent of distance. These various cost elements may or may not be reflected in the market prices of different journeys. A similar situation may be expected to hold in the case of goods transport, a matter discussed in section 6 below.

A common method of treating a simple aspect of the quality problem can be applied when goods are graded say by size or weight. Thus eggs are frequently graded by size and large ones, other things being equal, cost more than small ones. If information were available about the number of eggs in each grade it would be possible to treat each grade as a separate commodity. This result could be reproduced exactly if there was an exact relationship between price and size (or weight) and if information were available about the average size (or weight) of eggs sold as well as about their number. Such information could be obtained by sampling methods without the necessity for detailed records of all quantities sold classified by grade.

Another method of handling the problem of quality differences is to rely on the construction of price index-numbers and to use these for the deflation of value changes. The advantage of this procedure lies in the fact that price movements for different varieties of a commodity which are made from similar materials by similar processes are likely to be very much alike. Thus the average price movement for the members of a class or sub-class of commodities may be approximated by an average of a limited number of quotations for goods of constant quality. If it becomes impossible to obtain price quotations for a particular specification or if this specification ceases to be representative of the varieties now traded it is necessary to shift to a new specification and in doing so to allow for any shift in quality involved. Precisely how this shift should be introduced depends in whether a base- or current-weighted price index is being constructed. Provided that the value of transactions is known at each date, a base-weighted price index requires only a knowledge of the parameters in the price-quality relationship in the current period whereas a current-weighted price index requires a knowledge of the corresponding parameters in the base period. Thus so far as this problem is concerned Λ (and P) are easier to construct than Π (and L) since when substitute specifications have to be introduced it is almost always necessary to assess (usually by reference to trade opinion) the money value of the quality difference between the old specification and the new at the time when the change-over takes place.

5. NEW MODELS AND NEW PRODUCTS

The forms of quality difference and variety change discussed so far merge imperceptibly into cases where the element of novelty introduced by the change is greater so that it becomes more and more difficult to accommodate the new product within the framework of relative values existing in the base period. A case intermediate between a mere change in variety such as the average strength of beer or the average size of eggs and a wholly new product is the appearance of new models. This problem arises in a wide range of products and is particularly noticeable in the case of motor cars which, accordingly, will be taken as an example.

In the last generation a large number of technical improvements have taken place in the design of motor cars with the result that they have become on the whole more reliable, more comfortable, of higher performance and cheaper to run. These changes have been introduced to the consuming public by the appearance, year after year, of new models which have incorporated various modifications of design so that, even for the same variety of the same type of car, models for succeeding years cannot be regarded as identical.

The problem of comparing different cars at the same time and over time can be solved if it is possible to relate prices to quality characteristics in the base period and if the same quality characteristics are adequate to describe the cars available in the current period.

It seems likely that a study of the prices and specifications of different models and types of car produced at particular times would yield satisfactory relationships between price and quality characteristics. On this subject reference should be made to a paper by Court [5] who many years ago emphasised the importance of prices in terms of specifications as a valid basis for price comparisons and applied ideas essentially similar to those set out above to the construction of a price index for motor-cars. This would provide a means of comparing different models and types in the base period. In moving to the current period two types of finding might be expected. First, technical change is almost certainly uneven in reducing the cost of improving different aspects of quality so that the weights of the different quality characteristics would probably change

57

over time. If this were in fact the case it would provide yet another example of the fundamental index-number problem. Second, if technical progress is rapid and if the base and current periods are far apart it is likely that the observations for the two periods will lie in more or less distinct regions of the quality space so that some hesitation may be felt in extrapolating the price-quality relationship found in one period to the conditions of the other. How far this situation is in fact commonly met with is a matter for investigation. If it is met with the problem of comparison can be seen to reduce to the problem of the prices which might have been expected in the base period for qualities which lay outside the range of those in fact available at the time.

If the comparison is made with a base period in the relatively distant past it may be expected that in the base period only very expensive cars had quality characteristics which later on became fairly general. From the point of view of such a base period technical improvements will be represented as producing a large rise in quality, and therefore quantity, and a large fall in price. To an extent which cannot be determined these tendencies may well be exaggerated since the very high prices of the superlative qualities of the base period are likely to be a reflexion of the low marginal utility of money of a very small group of very rich buyers. From the producer's point of view this is no objection but from the average consumers' point of view it may be considered to lead to an exaggeration of the fall in price and the rise in quality.

If a comparison with the past is made from a base period in the present it may be expected that the poorer qualities of the past will not be reflected in the observations of the base period. If these poorer qualities were due to less inputs (materials, workmanship, etc.) it might be reasonable to suppose that they would be both produced and bought at prices similar to those derivable from the base-period (contemporary) price-quality relationship. A more likely situation is one in which the inputs are similar but improvements in design have led to improvements in quality. In this case the cost of the old-fashioned article might not be very different from the present cost but the price which present consumers would pay for it would be altogether lower. Such a situation would account for the fact that the poorer quality of the past was now no longer produced.

This discussion of new models brings out the fact that their treatment becomes difficult to the extent that they cannot be fitted into the price-quality relationship of the base period without a considerable extrapolation of base-period experience. From this point of view the distinction between quality changes and new products can be expressed in precisely these terms. A quality change is a change in product which can be accommodated within the base-period system of values; a new product involves a change which cannot be so accommodated. The extent to which new models fall mainly into one or other of these categories depends ultimately on experience but it is also influenced by the quality characteristics in terms of which commodities are described. This is a matter which, to some extent, is in the control of the investigator in the sense that there are certainly ways of describing commodities which form a very inadequate basis for comparison.

This last remark can be illustrated by an attempt to introduce motor cars into a comparison with a past period in which only horse-drawn vehicles were available. In terms of an ordinary commodity classification, horses and carriages on the one hand and motor cars on the other are clearly distinct commodities which cannot be directly compared. Each however is concerned with the provision of transport services in which elements of speed, comfort, reliability, economy of maintenance, etc. enter. In the base period the prices of the various means of achieving these constituents of transport service may be expressible in terms of them. For early motor cars the range of variability of these characteristics may not be widely different from that of horse-drawn vehicles in which case a basis of comparison exists. Modern motor cars possess certain characteristics to an extent which lies altogether outside the range encountered in the above comparison and so they could hardly be fitted into the same scheme.

This discussion, necessarily tentative and hypothetical, brings out the basic reason why short-term comparisons are likely to prove more manageable than long-term comparisons. The latter, it would seem, can only be made by means of a chain of intermediate comparisons. If this is done, however, it has to be recognised that in the intermediate links the system of relative values is constantly changing.

6. CHARGES WHICH ARE NOT PROPORTIONAL TO QUANTITY

A large part of this chapter has been taken up with the discussion, in various contexts, of the basic principle that, wherever the question is important, commodities should be so defined that one unit has a single price in each period independently of other circumstances. The main objective in these discussions has been so to arrange matters that for each separately distinguished commodity the expenditure on that commodity shall, at any one time, be proportional to the quantity bought.

There are a number of cases in practice where this result will be prevented by the method of charging adopted unless special steps are taken. These cases are characterised by the fact the price is a function of the quantity bought in terms of the unit of quantity in which the transaction is carried out. Examples of this situation are two-part tariffs, frequently used as a basis for gas and electricity charges, most transport charges for goods, which involve an allowance for loading and unloading expenses that is independent of distance, and rebates for bulk purchases.

Consider a two-part tariff for the payment for electric current whereby the consumer pays a fixed charge, often based on the size of his establishment, plus a variable charge which is proportional to the number of units of current which he consumes. Under this system the average (but not the marginal) cost of a unit of current varies with the amount used by the consumer. Accordingly if the amount of current is the only quantity considered its price will change if the average consumption per consumer changes even though the fixed charge and the variable unit charge remain unaltered. It also follows that the average price of this commodity in any period depends on the way in which its consumption is distributed among consumers.

These awkward results can be avoided if the total amounts of the fixed and variable charges are known in the base period. The expenditure on the fixed charge can then be associated with the number of consumers (multiplied, if appropriate, by the sizes of their establishments) and the expenditure on the variable charge can be associated with the amount of current consumed. This treatment is equivalent to the introduction of two commodities in place of one. The second of these may be described as the right to draw on the public supply of electricity and is associated with the fixed part of the charge.

A similar treatment could be applied to many kinds of transportation charge which are usually so fixed that they contain a considerable element of fixed charge to cover, in the case of goods, loading and unloading costs which are independent of the distance covered and a variable charge depending on distance. Although it is usual to measure goods transportation services in ton-miles it would be more appropriate to say that the understanding between the buyer and the seller is that the goods shall not only be carried for a given distance but that they shall also be loaded and unloaded. Effect can be given to this understanding if the service of transportation is divided into two commodities. The first of these is the service of loading and unloading measured in tons with a weight equal to the value of the fixed part of the charge. The second is the service of carriage measured in ton-miles with a weight equal to the value of the variable part of the charge.

Another problem which could be resolved by replacing a single commodity by two commodities is that of discounts for large orders. The weight to be applied to the indicator of the commodity in the ordinary sense, say steel, would be the quantity in the base year multiplied by the price chargeable for the largest orders. The remainder of the weight would be applied to an indicator of the use made of the right to buy in small lots which, with only two sizes of lot, large and small, could be taken as the number of small purchases. While this possibility exists it is doubtful if it would be worthwhile to apply it in practice.

V

INTERMEDIATE SERVICES
AND ROUTING PROBLEMS

1. DIFFERENTIAL PRICES AND INTERMEDIATE SERVICES

At any one time quality differences are likely to account for a large part of the observed differences in price among the different varieties of a commodity. On the other hand identical varieties may vary considerably in price if they are bought in different localities or in different types of retail outlet. These differences are due to variations in intermediate services attaching to the physical commodities and their treatment forms the subject of this chapter.

This kind of problem is exemplified by the localisation of production and consumption and the existence of transport services which enable goods produced in one locality to be consumed in another. In general agricultural produce costs less in the rural areas where it is produced than in the towns to which much of it is transported, coal costs less at the pithead than elsewhere and many manufactured goods, such as motor cars, cost less at their place of manufacture than in distant areas to which freight and handling charges are considerable.

Since by hypothesis the goods in these examples may be regarded as identical in the different localities it is sometimes maintained that they should be given equal weights in quantity index-numbers or, equivalently, that they should be treated as if they had everywhere the same price in the base period. If this view is accepted there arises the question of which price to adopt; for example should it be the city price or the rural price or some average of base period prices in the various localities. The view taken in this Report is that the existence of price differentials should lead to the presumption that apparently similar commodities in fact differ in some respect which should be reflected in index-numbers of prices and quantities and indeed may be likened to a quality difference.

The proposal made here accords with the social accounting convention that the home-grown produce consumed by farm families should be valued at farm prices, that is at the price which the farmer could get for his produce if he sold it instead of consuming it. Since similar produce when sold on the market to other final consumers is valued at

61

retail prices, this treatment insures that a given quantity of potatoes, say, will count for more if it is consumed in a town rather than on the farm and consequently that an increase in the proportion of a given quantity of potatoes consumed in towns will, other things being equal, raise an index of final expenditure in real terms. Such a shift will always take place, on the principles adopted in this Report, if there is a movement towards varieties which had larger net output contents (or higher prices) in the base period.

This treatment involves an acceptance for valuation purposes of prices as they actually were in the base period and imputations based on the alternatives actually facing the transactors concerned. There is no room in this conception for the notion of the cost of urbanism in the sense of the additional expense incurred by townsfolk in acquiring agricultural produce. Similarly there is no room for the notion of the cost of not living at a centre of motor car production in the sense of the additional expense incurred by the inhabitants of, say, San Francisco in comparison with those in Detroit in acquiring a new motor car. Consequently it cannot be said, on the present view, that what people really want is potatoes and motor cars but not transport because in fact this possibility is not open to them or, if it is, they do not choose it. It seems quite likely that in a dynamic world the cost-minimising activities of producers and consumers do not result in a continuous state of equilibrium in which resources are always distributed in an optimum manner. But it seems very doubtful whether index-numbers of prices and quantities could be improved by attempting to go behind observed values and the actual possibilities open to transactors.

What has been said above about transport could equally be applied to distribution. Many shops selling fruit and vegetables for example offer advantages in such matters as quality, choice and delivery services which are not available to the purchaser who gets his fruit and vegetables from a street barrow just before closing time on a Saturday evening. In principle the difference in prices (in the base period) should be taken into account in the construction of quantity index-numbers. In practice, of course, it is usually quite impossible to collect price information in such detail and the assumption that would justify the failure to do so is that the relative quantities bought through the various forms of retail outlet have not changed significantly over the period of comparison.

It is, however, possible that for some purposes what is required is a comparison of certain elements of final product in two periods rather than of the two final products as a whole. Thus, in terms of the above example, the problem may be to compare the amount of potatoes consumed without taking account of the transport and distribution services associated with them which may be quite different in the two periods. Comparisons of this kind may also be useful in comparing the standard of living of different categories of consumer, such as urban and rural workers, since standards of living are frequently thought of in terms of goods and direct services alone. Thus it might be argued that what is important, in terms of the present example, in comparing urban and rural workers is the relative amounts of potatoes they consume and that the comparison would be distorted if the trade and transport services required to enable the urban worker to consume potatoes were counted in as well.

This line of thought could be interpreted as placing trade and goods transport outside the boundary of production to be accounted for. It is not, however, necessary to go as far as this since there is no difficulty in taking these activities into account, as must be done for many purposes, and in then ignoring their contribution in making certain comparisons. An example of the various ways in which this might be done is set out in section 3 below after the question of the routing of commodity flows has been discussed.

Even if the foregoing arguments are granted, difficulties still remain. These are associated with the practical problem of drawing a wholly satisfactory production boundary and of distinguishing correctly in practice between income and business expense. Thus, for example, it is usual to treat all travel undertaken and paid for by private consumers as a part of final product. To the extent that a part of the travel is regarded as a business expense the measure of product may come to depend in part on institutional arrangements so that comparisons will be disturbed if these arrangements change.

Since the information provided by index-numbers is always relative to a base period it is the relative values in this period which are relevant. Thus, for example, if a motor car factory were set up in the San Francisco area which could produce cars there as cheaply as at the factories in Detroit then this event will result in a fall in the price of cars in San Francisco relative to the earlier base period and not in a fall in quantity. Similarly if a coal strike in certain areas means that a large town has to be supplied from more distant pits and therefore, for a time, to pay higher prices for coal this event will result in a rise in the price of coal in that town and not in a rise in quantity.

2. THE ROUTING OF COMMODITY FLOWS

The preceding sections will have made clear the attitude adopted in this Report towards the treatment of quality differences and of differences in the intermediate services which attach to goods. It is convenient at this point to discuss the technical question of the routing of commodity flows through an accounting system. The various possibilities available differ mainly in the treatment of transport and distributive services and considerable care is needed if the way in which the commodity flows are routed is not to influence the index numbers of prices and quantities. The obvious possibilities may briefly be described as follows.

The first method involves routing the commodities through the accounting structure in such a way as to reproduce the course which

63

they actually take. Thus if transactor A buys a commodity from transactor B, the transaction is shown in full as a debit to the appropriate account of A and as a credit to the appropriate account of B. This method, though straightforward in one sense, will involve the passage of many commodities one or more times through the distributive system on their way from producer to consumer. It will also require in many cases distinctions between what appear physically similar commodities as they pass from producer to consumer if differences and changes in intermediate services are to have any effect of the index-numbers. Thus for example no distinctions need to be made among the motor cars of identical specification made at a certain factory since each will have the same base-year value. But, especially in a large country, some distinction should be made between various groups of these physically similar cars depending on the fact that retail prices vary with place of purchase. In principle wherever base-year unit values are different sub-groups of this kind should be formed. In practice, however, as already mentioned, the availability of data and the work involved are likely to set severe limits to the formation of such sub-groups. In any case their formation will only be important if the quantity movements for the sub-groups are neither similar nor offsetting.

The two other routing methods now to be considered are artificial in the sense that they involve splitting up transactions into constituent parts in a way which does not usually happen in the actual world. Such methods are adopted in the construction of input-output tables where it is important that the technological connections between sectors should be preserved. This would be difficult, if not impossible, with the first routing method since nearly every commodity would continually be passing through a distributive sector after which the identity of its source would be lost.

Accordingly the second method, which is in fact the one usually employed in the construction of input-output tables, is to treat each good as sold to its user (whether intermediate or final) at producer's prices and to treat each added service, such as transport or distribution, as the object of a separate sale. On this basis producers are shown as buying commodities directly from one another even if the transaction in fact takes place through a wholesaler or other distributor. The purchaser is then assumed to make a separate purchase of transport and distributive services, if any, so that the total amount he pays for the commodities he buys is distributed over the producers of goods and services who combine to get these commodities to him. Similarly, all services, such as transport and distribution, in connection with final goods appear explicitly as final purchases in their own right.

With this method it is no longer necessary to separate physically similar goods into categories according to their base-period values. Thus for example all motor cars, wherever the buyer may be, are sold to their ultimate purchasers at factory values. But this simplification is offset by the fact that intermediate services attaching to final goods now become final services and must be properly defined and measured even if all that is required is an index of total product without any subdivision by industry. However, just because this method accords with the usual conventions of input-output analysis it is likely that in many countries large masses of data will come to be arranged in this way and it would be convenient if they could be adapted to the present needs as well.

The third method, like the second, also involves an artificial or conventional treatment of the cost of intermediate services. In this case, however, such services, instead of being treated as sold separately to the buyer of the good, are treated as sold separately to the seller who is assumed to sell at the price, inclusive of the cost of the services, actually paid by the buyer.

This method has the advantage compared with the second that no part of intermediate services appears directly in final product, and compared with the first that to a considerable extent at any rate the technological links between industries are maintained. It is not, however, in general use as a means of arranging social accounting data. Like the second method it is less direct for present purposes than the first method and involves difficulties in constructing production index-numbers for separate industries.

The kinds of problem to which these methods give rise can perhaps best be seen by an example. The following illustration is intentionally kept exceedingly simple and does not exemplify all the problems that arise.

Let it be assumed that there is an economy composed of three industries, agriculture, transport and distribution, and final consumers. All problems connected with capital formation, government and foreign transactions are excluded. Agriculture produces a single, homogeneous, good, say potatoes, its only inputs being factor services. Distribution undertakes the buying of the potatoes from agriculture and their sale to the consumers. Its inputs consist of potatoes and transport services as well as the services of factors of production.

The commodity flows in this economy at base-period values are represented in the transaction matrix V_{00} where

$$V_{00} \equiv \hat{p}_0 \, Q_0 \qquad\qquad (5.1)$$

In (5.1), $\hat{p}_0$ denotes a diagonal matrix with the base-period prices of the outputs of the three industries in the leading diagonal. It is assumed that the farm price of potatoes is 1 per unit, that transportation costs 1 per unit of the service and that the retail price of potatoes is 1.5 per unit. In a similar way Q_0 denotes a matrix of base-period commodity inputs and outputs measured in quantity units. Agriculture produces a hundred units (say tons) of potatoes, transport produces ten units (say ton-miles) of transport services and distribution distributes a hundred units (say tons) of transported potatoes. The same amount of transport services enters into each ton of potatoes.

Method 1. These assumptions permit (5.1) to be given a specific numerical interpretation. Thus, on method 1,

$$\begin{bmatrix} 0 & 0 & 100 & 0 \\ 0 & 0 & 10 & 0 \\ 0 & 0 & 0 & 150 \end{bmatrix} = \begin{bmatrix} 1 & 0 & 0 \\ 0 & 1 & 0 \\ 0 & 0 & 1.5 \end{bmatrix} \begin{bmatrix} 0 & 0 & 100 & 0 \\ 0 & 0 & 10 & 0 \\ 0 & 0 & 0 & 100 \end{bmatrix} \quad (5.2)$$

In the current period, agriculture produces a hundred units of potatoes, transport produces 11 units of transport services but owing to the longer distance travelled 10 per cent of the crop is wasted so that distribution distributes 90 units of potatoes with an input of 100 units of potatoes and 11 units of transport services in addition to the services of factors of production. Thus, if V_{01} denotes the commodity flow matrix in the current period at base-period values,

$$V_{01} = \hat{p}_0 Q_1 \quad (5.3)$$

or, in numerical terms,

$$\begin{bmatrix} 0 & 0 & 100 & 0 \\ 0 & 0 & 11 & 0 \\ 0 & 0 & 0 & 135 \end{bmatrix} = \begin{bmatrix} 1 & 0 & 0 \\ 0 & 1 & 0 \\ 0 & 0 & 1.5 \end{bmatrix} \begin{bmatrix} 0 & 0 & 100 & 0 \\ 0 & 0 & 11 & 0 \\ 0 & 0 & 0 & 90 \end{bmatrix} \quad (5.4)$$

The Laspeyres index-numbers of quantity, L say, for each industry can be obtained by subtracting the sum of the items in the appropriate column from the sum of the items in the corresponding row of V_{01} and by dividing this total by the corresponding total derived from V_{00}. The Laspeyres quantity index-number for the economy as a whole can be obtained by dividing the sum of the numerators of the individual industry ratios by the sum of their denominators or, alternatively, as the ratio of the sum of the entries in the final columns of V_{01} and V_{00}. Thus

			L
Agriculture	100/100	=	1.0
Transport	11/10	=	1.1
Distribution	(135-100-11)/(150-100-10)	=	0.6
Total	135/150	=	0.9

These results should appear intuitively acceptable. Thus, without any quality changes, the quantity of the final good (potatoes) has fallen by 10 per cent, and this is shown in the aggregate production index. There are no inputs from other industries into agriculture or transport and the gross output of these industries remains unchanged and rises by 10 per cent respectively. The net output of distribution falls since it distributes a smaller quantity of potatoes with the same input from the growers and a larger input from the transport industry.

66

Method 2. On this method each industry sells the whole of its net output direct to consumers in the base period. Thus to (5.2) there corresponds

$$\begin{bmatrix} 0 & 0 & 0 & 100 \\ 0 & 0 & 0 & 10 \\ 0 & 0 & 0 & 40 \end{bmatrix} = \begin{bmatrix} 1 & 0 & 0 \\ 0 & 1 & 0 \\ 0 & 0 & 0.4 \end{bmatrix} \begin{bmatrix} 0 & 0 & 0 & 100 \\ 0 & 0 & 0 & 10 \\ 0 & 0 & 0 & 100 \end{bmatrix} \quad (5.5)$$

If this method is to give the same results as method 1 it has to be recognised that in the current period not only is 10 per cent of the potato crop lost in the distributive system but that two units of transportation also suffer a similar fate. Thus, on this method, V_{01} appears as

$$\begin{bmatrix} 0 & 0 & 10 & 90 \\ 0 & 0 & 2 & 9 \\ 0 & 0 & 0 & 36 \end{bmatrix} = \begin{bmatrix} 1 & 0 & 0 \\ 0 & 1 & 0 \\ 0 & 0 & 0.4 \end{bmatrix} \begin{bmatrix} 0 & 0 & 10 & 90 \\ 0 & 0 & 2 & 9 \\ 0 & 0 & 0 & 90 \end{bmatrix} \quad (5.6)$$

A combination of (5.5) and (5.6) gives the following values for the index-numbers

			L
Agriculture	(10+90)/100	=	1.0
Transport	(2+9)/10	=	1.1
Distribution	(36-10-2)/40	=	0.6
Total	135/150	=	0.9

It will be seen that the information needed to allocate the sales of agriculture and transport under method 2 was also necessary in the application of method 1. The essential facts are that in the current period 10 per cent of the potato crop went to waste after leaving the growers and that there was no change in the quality of the distributed part despite the increased volume of transport services.

Method 3. On this method transport and distribution sell the whole of their services to agriculture in the base period and agriculture sells the potatoes to the consumers at retail prices. Thus to (5.2) there corresponds

$$\begin{bmatrix} 0 & 0 & 0 & 150 \\ 10 & 0 & 0 & 0 \\ 40 & 0 & 0 & 0 \end{bmatrix} = \begin{bmatrix} 1.5 & 0 & 0 \\ 0 & 1 & 0 \\ 0 & 0 & 0.4 \end{bmatrix} \begin{bmatrix} 0 & 0 & 0 & 100 \\ 10 & 0 & 0 & 0 \\ 100 & 0 & 0 & 0 \end{bmatrix} \quad (5.7)$$

If this method is to give the same results as method 1 it is again necessary to recognise that part of the crop is wasted in the current period and that the additional transport services in that period do nothing to increase final product. Thus, on this method, V_{01} appears as

$$\begin{bmatrix} 0 & 0 & 15 & 135 \\ 10 & 0 & 1 & 0 \\ 40 & 0 & 0 & 0 \end{bmatrix} = \begin{bmatrix} 1.5 & 0 & 0 \\ 0 & 1 & 0 \\ 0 & 0 & 0.4 \end{bmatrix} \begin{bmatrix} 0 & 0 & 10 & 90 \\ 10 & 0 & 1 & 0 \\ 100 & 0 & 0 & 0 \end{bmatrix} \quad (5.8)$$

A combination of (5.7) and (5.8) gives the following values for the index-numbers:

		L
Agriculture	$(15+135-10-40)/(150-10-40)=$	1.0
Transport	$(10+1)/10$ =	1.1
Distribution	$(40-15-1)/40$ =	0.6
Total	$135/150$ =	0.9

Again the index-numbers are the same as in method 1. So far as the index of total product is concerned this result follows provided that only 90 per cent of the crop is shown as sold by agriculture to consumers. If the question of routing is regarded as a purely formal matter so that the industries are assumed to perform the same functions in production independently of the method of routing then the remaining 10 per cent of the crop must be treated as sold by agriculture to distribution and the sales of transport services must be shown as in (5.8). If on the other hand transport and distribution were regarded as merely subsidiary activities to agriculture and not as independent industries then it would be appropriate to shift the expenses shown in the third columns of V_{01} and Q_{01} in (5.8) back into the first column. If this is done the production movements in agriculture and distribution will be interchanged. This example shows the need for clarity as regards the functions which entities called industries perform if the component index-numbers are to be capable of interpretation.

3. PARTIAL COMPARISONS

In the preceding section the final product was distributed potatoes and it was shown (i) that each routing method, when properly applied, led to the same set of index-numbers and (ii) that the index of final product was equal to the change in the quantity of distributed potatoes. This result followed because, in the base period, all potatoes required the same amount of trade and transport services to enable them to reach the consumer. But this condition will not be satisfied if a distinction is drawn between farm consumers for whom no trade and transport services are necessary and others for whom they are. How, it may be asked, will the three routing systems work out in a case like this?

In order to keep the numerical example simple it will be assumed that, as before, there are only three industries, agriculture, transport and trade. The products are also the same as before but there are now two types of consumer, the farmer and the towndweller. Trade and transport services are needed to get potatoes to the towndweller but not to get them to the farmer.

In period 0, the crop of 100 units of potatoes is divided equally between the two classes of consumer. The farm price is one per unit. Transport requirements, also valued at one per unit, amount to 0.2 units per unit of potatoes distributed to towndwellers. The retail price of potatoes in towns is 1.5 per unit. In period 1, 80 out of the 100 units of potatoes produced are consumed in towns.

On this basis, the results obtained from the different methods may be set out as follows.

Method 1. The numerical values corresponding to (5.1) and (5.3) are

$$
\begin{bmatrix} 0 & 0 & 50 & 50 \\ 0 & 0 & 10 & 0 \\ 0 & 0 & 0 & 75 \end{bmatrix} = \begin{bmatrix} 1 & 0 & 0 \\ 0 & 1 & 0 \\ 0 & 0 & 1.5 \end{bmatrix} \begin{bmatrix} 0 & 0 & 50 & 50 \\ 0 & 0 & 10 & 0 \\ 0 & 0 & 0 & 50 \end{bmatrix} \quad (5.9)
$$

and

$$
\begin{bmatrix} 0 & 0 & 80 & 20 \\ 0 & 0 & 16 & 0 \\ 0 & 0 & 0 & 120 \end{bmatrix} = \begin{bmatrix} 1 & 0 & 0 \\ 0 & 1 & 0 \\ 0 & 0 & 1.5 \end{bmatrix} \begin{bmatrix} 0 & 0 & 80 & 20 \\ 0 & 0 & 16 & 0 \\ 0 & 0 & 0 & 80 \end{bmatrix} \quad (5.10)
$$

From these data the index-numbers are

		L
Agriculture	$(80+20)/(50+50)$	$= 1.00$
Transport	$16/10$	$= 1.60$
Distribution	$(120-80-16)/(75-50-10)$	$= 1.60$
Total	$(20+120)/(50+75)$	$= 1.12$

Thus the index of final product has risen by 12 per cent although the amount of potatoes produced and consumed has remained unchanged. The reason for this is that the move to the towns has increased the level of production in trade and transport. Since, by assumption no one is compelled to live in the towns it may be assumed that the community prefer situation 1 to any alternative and in particular to the alternative of remaining in their original numbers on the farms and producing the larger number of potatoes which the growth of transport and distribution services would presumably have made possible in that period.

However, if living standards are measured by potatoes consumed, there is clearly no change between the two periods. This is obvious from the data but does not emerge clearly from the accounting statements at constant prices indicated on the left-hand sides of (5.9) and (5.10). It is fortuitous that the net output of agriculture is unchanged since, for present purposes, standards of living are to be measured by the gross output of agriculture reaching consumers. The comparison required is, however, brought out clearly by method 2.

Method 2. The numerical values corresponding to (5.1) and (5.3) are

$$\begin{bmatrix} 0 & 0 & 0 & 100 \\ 0 & 0 & 0 & 10 \\ 0 & 0 & 0 & 15 \end{bmatrix} = \begin{bmatrix} 1 & 0 & 0 \\ 0 & 1 & 0 \\ 0 & 0 & 0.3 \end{bmatrix} \begin{bmatrix} 0 & 0 & 0 & 100 \\ 0 & 0 & 0 & 10 \\ 0 & 0 & 0 & 50 \end{bmatrix} \quad (5.11)$$

and

$$\begin{bmatrix} 0 & 0 & 0 & 100 \\ 0 & 0 & 0 & 16 \\ 0 & 0 & 0 & 24 \end{bmatrix} = \begin{bmatrix} 1 & 0 & 0 \\ 0 & 1 & 0 \\ 0 & 0 & 0.3 \end{bmatrix} \begin{bmatrix} 0 & 0 & 0 & 100 \\ 0 & 0 & 0 & 16 \\ 0 & 0 & 0 & 80 \end{bmatrix} \quad (5.12)$$

whence the following index-numbers may be calculated

		L
Agriculture	100/100	= 1.00
Transport	16/10	= 1.60
Distribution	24/15	= 1.60
Total	(100+16+24)/(100+10+15) =	1.12

In this case the comparison of standards of living in terms of potatoes emerges at once from the left-hand sides of (5.11) and (5.12); it is necessary only to compare the final entries in the first rows. This result would equally follow if the table recorded a large number of different commodities produced in different places since in each case the part of output which reached consumers would be shown at producers' prices. Trade and transport activities are accounted for in this arrangement but they are not brought into the particular comparison under discussion.

Method 3 is not useful for present purposes and, in applying it, it is necessary to divide agriculture between subsistence agriculture and production for the (town) market. If subsistence agriculture, A_1, is shown in the first row and column, the numerical values corresponding to (5.1) and (5.3) are

$$\begin{bmatrix} 0 & 0 & 0 & 0 & 50 \\ 0 & 0 & 0 & 0 & 75 \\ 0 & 10 & 0 & 0 & 0 \\ 0 & 15 & 0 & 0 & 0 \end{bmatrix} = \begin{bmatrix} 1 & 0 & 0 & 0 \\ 0 & 1.5 & 0 & 0 \\ 0 & 0 & 1 & 0 \\ 0 & 0 & 0 & 0.3 \end{bmatrix} \begin{bmatrix} 0 & 0 & 0 & 0 & 50 \\ 0 & 0 & 0 & 0 & 50 \\ 0 & 10 & 0 & 0 & 0 \\ 0 & 50 & 0 & 0 & 0 \end{bmatrix} \quad (5.13)$$

and

$$\begin{bmatrix} 0 & 0 & 0 & 0 & 20 \\ 0 & 0 & 0 & 0 & 120 \\ 0 & 16 & 0 & 0 & 0 \\ 0 & 24 & 0 & 0 & 0 \end{bmatrix} = \begin{bmatrix} 1 & 0 & 0 & 0 \\ 0 & 1.5 & 0 & 0 \\ 0 & 0 & 1 & 0 \\ 0 & 0 & 0 & 0.3 \end{bmatrix} \begin{bmatrix} 0 & 0 & 0 & 0 & 10 \\ 0 & 0 & 0 & 0 & 80 \\ 0 & 16 & 0 & 0 & 0 \\ 0 & 80 & 0 & 0 & 0 \end{bmatrix} \quad (5.14)$$

whence the following index-numbers may be calculated

		L
A_1	20/50	= 0.40
A_2	(120—16—24)/(75—10—15)	= 1.60
Agriculture	100/100	= 1.00
Transport	16/10	= 1.60
Distribution	24/15	= 1.60
Total	(20+120)/(50+75)	= 1.12

The purpose of this section is to show (i) that partial comparisons can be accommodated within the general framework set out in this Report and (ii) that the particular type of comparison considered is simplified if the data are arranged as in method 2. This being so, no useful purpose would be served by narrowing the general framework so as to lead exclusively to this type of partial comparison.

VI

SEASONAL VARIATIONS

1. INTRODUCTION

All that is said in this Report about seasonal differences and their adjustment is concentrated in this chapter despite the fact that the subject involves in part a continuation of the discussion of the conceptual problems of the preceding chapters and in part a discussion of the practical problems of measurement which is otherwise concentrated in the chapter VIII. The reasons for this are that seasonal variations form an important and interesting subject and that an attempt will be made here to give it a systematic treatment which would not fit well into a section of a chapter dealing largely with other matters. In view of the amount that has already been written on the subject some further explanation may be helpful at the outset.

The usual methods of seasonal adjustment are designed to extract from the observations a normal seasonal pattern by means of which they can be adjusted so as to show their movement over time free of regular seasonal influences. These methods do not go into questions of causation and so the first point to establish is whether or not, on some suitable hypothesis as to the effect of the unexamined seasonal influences, there is or is not a significant difference between seasons. If there is, the average effect of seasonal influences in each season is measured and the observations are adjusted accordingly.

In the case of quantity series it is usually recognised that certain irregular influences of a seasonal character ought to be taken into account. The first of these is the irregular effective time period (working days) which carry the same seasonal label in different years. The second is the existence of moveable feasts such as Easter and Whitsun which occur once and only in each year but not always at the same time.

If differences in the effective length of the time periods to which the observations relate is for the moment ignored, it can be seen that the remaining aspects of the subject so far discussed can be treated as a problem in the analysis of variance and therefore as a problem of regression on dummy variables. The extraction of a normal seasonal pattern requires a set of dummy variables equal in number to the number of seasons each of which indicates the presence or absence of a particular

73

season at the time of each observation. The adjustment for moveable feasts requires a set of dummy variables equal in number to the number of moveable feasts each of which indicates the presence or absence of a particular moveable feast at the time of each observation.

In some cases it may be possible to go beyond a treatment in terms of the presence or absence of certain states and to consider the effect of variable causal influences. Thus, for example, in the Northern Hemisphere electricity consumption is seasonally high in January largely because the weather tends to be cold and the days tend to be dark in that month. If the coldness and darkness of January days were constant from year to year the whole effect of these influences could be extracted by means of the dummy variables just discussed. But in fact such influences vary from year to year and may in fact be largely responsible for irregularities in seasonal movements. If the relevant variable influences can be introduced it will be possible to refine the treatment of seasonal influences and to produce an adjusted series which reflects more closely the movement of the underlying series as it would be if conditions were constant from observation to observation. This further step can be formulated in terms of regression on actual as well as dummy variables. As more relevant actual variables are introduced the analysis provides more explanation as opposed to mere description of seasonal changes.

Since all these problems can be formulated in terms of the well-known techniques of regression analysis it is possible to set up a general system of regression models appropriate to various hypotheses about seasonal influences and to varying amounts of available data. It is also possible in this way to bring the problems of seasonal adjustment into relation with statistical notions of significance and efficient estimation.

Finally, a technique which is precisely equivalent to seasonal adjustment is relevant to another problem often met with in the analysis of time series which may be important for the purpose of this Report. It frequently happens that information is available in the form of a set of seasonal chains with no common base and it may be required to form out of these separate chains a continuous series by means of which comparisons between different seasons as well as between the same season in different years can be made. This subject finds a natural place in a theory of seasonal variations.

2. THE TREATMENT OF SEASONAL COMMODITIES

As a consequence of seasonal influences many commodities which appear similar in a physical sense are available in different quantities and sell at different prices at different times of the year. If the price differences occurred at the same time it would be desirable, in accordance with the treatment suggested in the preceding two chapters, to try to take them into account by treating the differently priced varieties as separate commodities. The existence of a regular seasonal pattern in prices which more or less repeats itself year after year suggests very strongly that the varieties of a commodity available at different seasons cannot be transformed into one another without cost and that, accordingly, in all cases where seasonal variations in price are significant, the varieties available at different times of the year should be treated, in principle, as separate commodities. This is equivalent to saying that season of availability is a quality characteristic unless there is no significant difference between the seasonal element of prices charged at different seasons.

If the varieties available at different seasons are treated as separate commodities then it would be possible, in the construction of annual quantity index-numbers, to include the quantity change between the base and current period for each season separately and to weight these changes by the appropriate seasonal expenditures. Thus, for example, if the index relates only to the seasonal varieties of a single commodity, then

$$L = \sum_s p_{s0}\, q_{s1} / \sum_s p_{s0}\, q_{s0} \qquad (6.1)$$

and so on. In this expression the suffix s ($s = 1, \ldots, m$) relates to a particular season out of the m seasons into which the year is divided.

This method is not satisfactory if one season is to be compared with the whole of a base year as in the construction of most monthly and quarterly index-numbers because the quantity units (for example 1bs or kgs) do not take into account seasonal quality differences and so are not comparable.

Consider the case in which the normal seasonal variation in prices can be represented by a set of multipliers, one for each season, so that the actual price, p_s in season s, is equal to the adjusted price, p_s^* times the multiplier for season s. Thus

$$\begin{aligned} p_s &= e^{\pi_s} p_s^* \\ &= \alpha_s p_s^* \end{aligned} \qquad (6.2)$$

where $1/\alpha_s$ is the seasonal adjustment for season s and since over a seasonal cycle, these adjustments must multiply out to unity $\sum_s \pi_s = 0$. If (6.2) is multiplied by q_s there results

$$\begin{aligned} p_s\, q_s &= p_s^*\, \alpha_s\, q_s \\ &= p_s^*\, q_s^* \end{aligned} \qquad (6.3)$$

say, where q_s^* provides a quantity measure in terms of which different seasons can be compared.

In these terms the Laspeyres quantity index is given by

$$\begin{aligned} L &= \sum_s p_{s0}^*\, q_{s1}^* / \sum_s p_{s0}^*\, q_{s0}^* \\ &= \sum_s p_{s0}\, q_{s1} / \sum_s p_{s0}\, q_{s0} \end{aligned} \qquad (6.4)$$

75

as in (6.1) since the adjustments to the price and quantity indicators cancel out for each season. If the mean adjusted price, $\bar{p}_0^*$, and the mean adjusted quantity, $\bar{q}_0^*$, in the base year are defined as

$$\bar{p}_0^* = \sum_s p_{so}^* \, q_{so}^* / \sum_s q_{so}^* \qquad (6.5)$$

and

$$\bar{q}_0^* = \sum_s q_{so}^* / m \qquad (6.6)$$

then the base-weighted quantity index can be written in the alternative form

$$L = \bar{p}_0^* \, \bar{q}_1^* / \bar{p}_0^* \, \bar{q}_0^*$$
$$= \sum_s q_{s1}^* / \sum_s q_{so}^* \qquad (6.7)$$

from (6.6). Equation (6.7) shows that in the adjusted quantity units, L is, in this case, a simple ratio of quantities. This is as it should be since in adjusted units the quantities of different seasons are directly comparable.

In these units a single season of one year can be compared with a different season or with a whole year. Thus if the comparison is between season s of year 1 and year 0 as a whole

$$L = \bar{p}_0^* \, q_{s1}^* / \bar{p}_0^* \, \bar{q}_0^*$$
$$= q_{s1}^* / \bar{q}_0^* \qquad (6.8)$$

Similarly, in this case

$$\Pi = p_{s1}^* \, q_{s1}^* / \bar{p}_0^* \, q_{s1}^*$$
$$= p_{s1}^* / \bar{p}_0^* \qquad (6.9)$$

whence, as is always the case with aggregative index-numbers

$$L\Pi = p_{s1}^* \, q_{s1}^* / \bar{p}_0^* \bar{q}_0^*$$
$$= V \qquad (6.10)$$

where V denotes the ratio of expenditure on the commodity in season s of year 1 to the average expenditure on the commodity in the base year.

It can be seen from (6.4) that if price and quantity information is available for each season then a correct annual comparison can be made without the need for seasonal adjustment. This result cannot, however, be obtained on the basis of annual averages. Thus let the unadjusted base-year averages of price and quantity, corresponding to (6.5) and (6.6), be given by

$$\bar{p}_0 = \sum_s p_{so} \, q_{so} / \sum_s q_{so} \qquad (6.11)$$

76

and

$$\bar{q}_0 = \sum_s q_{so}/m \qquad (6.12)$$

Then,

$$\bar{p}_0\,\bar{q}_1\,/\,\bar{p}_0\,\bar{q}_0 = \sum_s q_{s1}/\sum_s q_{so} \qquad (6.13)$$

which may be compared with (6.7).

The unsatisfactory nature of (6.13) as a measure of the quantity change between the two years can be readily be seen by an example. Suppose the commodity to be one which in the base year is available in substantial quantities for only a small part of the year but can be purchased at a very high price in other parts of the year. By the time the current year is reached the development of alternative sources of supply, refrigeration, etc. has made the commodity available in more or less equal quantities throughout the year. The use of adjusted measures, as in (6.7), reflects the fact that something is now available which was valued very highly in the base year, namely " out of season " varieties of the commodity. The use of unadjusted measures, as in (6.13), does not reflect this fact. Equation (6.4) shows that this last result does not conform with that obtained from the use of detailed seasonal information even in unadjusted form.

The argument of this section brings out two points. In the first place if, when the price is seasonally high, consumption is seasonally low then the provision of cheap " out of season " supplies will appear as a larger quantity increase from the base-year point of view than it will from the current-year point of view. In the second place if comparisons are required between seasons rather than between years then the estimation of the normal seasonal variation of prices appropriate to the base year forms an integral part of the calculations.

3. A METHOD OF SEASONAL ADJUSTMENT

The purpose of this and the following sections is to put forward a systematic method of performing seasonal adjustments starting with cases in which only a simple hypothesis can be advanced about the nature of seasonal variations and in which nothing is known about the factors responsible for these variations and going on to cases in which at least some of these factors can be specified and measured.

Consider, in the first instance, a trendless time series. Suppose that each year is divided into the same m seasons each of equal duration and that information is available in respect of each season for each of n years. The simplest hypothesis is that each season is, on the average, above or below the average for the series as a whole by a certain amount, positive or negative. These average magnitudes constitute the normal seasonal variation of the series and their subtraction season by season, from the original series will provide a seasonally adjusted series. This adjusted series will be acceptable if the hypothesis is acceptable.

77

If y_{st} denotes the element of the series which occurs in season s of year t, then the above hypothesis can be expressed in the form

$$y_{st} = \alpha + \beta_s + \varepsilon_{st} \qquad (6.14)$$

In (6.14) α denotes the true mean of the whole series, β_s denotes the excess over α of the true mean for season s and ε_{st} denotes a true residual. It is necessary to frame the hypothesis in such a way that a residual is explicitly included since it is not supposed that it will fit all the observations exactly and so it cannot be upset by the discovery of minor discrepancies.

Provided that the ε_{st} are independently distributed with constant variance the problem of estimating the general mean α and the m mean seasonal deviations, β_s, from the general mean can be put in the following form. It is required to minimise the sum of the squares of the true residuals, namely $\sum_s \sum_t \varepsilon_{st}^2$, subject to the condition that $\sum_s \beta_s = 0$. This condition ensures that the sum of the seasonal adjustments, the $-\beta_s$, is zero in any year but some such condition is necessary in any case because it is impossible to determine a set of seasonal means and a general mean independently since the general mean is simply the mean of the seasonal means and so is determined when they are known.

Let $\alpha + \beta_s = \gamma_s$. Then (6.14) can be seen to decompose into m separate equations each of which involves a single γ_s. If c_s is the least squares estimator of γ_s, then

$$c_s = \sum_t y_{st}/n$$
$$= \bar{y}_s \qquad (6.15)$$

where y_s is the mean of the observations for season s. Given the c_s then a, the estimator of α, is given by

$$\sum_s c_s/m = \sum_s \sum_t y_{st}/mn$$
$$= \bar{y} \qquad (6.16)$$

where $\bar{y}$ is the general mean of the observations. The estimator b_s of β_s is then given by

$$b_s = c_s - \sum_s c_s/m$$
$$= \bar{y}_s - \bar{y} \qquad (6.17)$$

The procedure just outlined is very simple and exhibits the problem of seasonal adjustment in terms of finding the excess of seasonal means over the general mean of the series. In this simple form, however, it would be of little practical value since it would apply only to trendless series. If the series to be analysed has a trend then successive seasonal means will differ on this account and they will reflect this trend as well as purely seasonal differences.

Before proceeding to this complication it is convenient to set out the method just described in terms of matrix algebra. A notation which is convenient for regression problems is given in Stone [21]. In the simple case there is little advantage in this way of presenting the problem but it is helpful in deriving the solution in more complex cases, in following the operations involved in different cases and in comparing the results. In matrix notation (6.14) may be written in the form

$$
\begin{aligned}
y &= i\,a + S\,\beta + \varepsilon \\
&= S\,(i_m\,a + \beta) + \varepsilon \\
&= S\gamma + \varepsilon
\end{aligned}
\tag{6.18}
$$

In (6.18) a has the same meaning as in (6.14), i and i_m denote respectively the unit vector with mn and with m elements, y, β and ε denote respectively vectors the elements of which are y_{st}, β_s and ε_{st} and S denotes a matrix of order $mn \times m$ which contains the unit matrix of order m repeated n times.

The least-squares estimator c of γ is

$$
c = (S'\,S)^{-1}\,S'\,y
\tag{6.19}
$$

Since, by definition, c must satisfy the relationship

$$
c = i_m\,a + b
\tag{6.20}
$$

and the estimator b of β must satisfy the condition

$$
i'_m\,b = 0
\tag{6.21}
$$

it follows that

$$
\begin{aligned}
a &= (i'_m\,i_m)^{-1}\,i'_m c \\
&= (i'i)^{-1}\,i'y
\end{aligned}
\tag{6.22}
$$

since by the definition of S

$$
(S'S)^{-1} = \frac{1}{n}\,I_m
\tag{6.23}
$$

and

$$
S\,i_m = i
\tag{6.24}
$$

By combining (6.19), (6.20) and (6.22) it can be seen that

$$
\begin{aligned}
b &= [I_m - i_m\,(i'_m i_m)^{-1} i'_m]\,(S'S)^{-1}S'y \\
&= (S'S)^{-1}\,S'\,[I - i\,(i'i)^{-1}i']\,y
\end{aligned}
\tag{6.25}
$$

The operator $(i'i)^{-1}i'$ applied to a vector is equivalent to taking the mean value of the elements of the vector. The operator $(S'S)^{-1}S'$ applied to a vector is equivalent, in terms of the present problem, to taking the set of seasonal means and arranging them in a vector. The expression $(S'S)^{-1}S'i$ is equal to i_m so that (6.25) shows that b is equal to the set of seasonal means adjusted for the general mean.

In order to decide whether any adjustment for seasonality should be made on the basis of the model it is necessary to test whether there is any significant variation associated specifically with seasons. This may be done by testing whether the variance of the seasonal means about the general mean is large compared with the variance of the observations each taken about its seasonal mean. The meaning of large, that is to say the level of significance adopted, has to be fixed conventionally, it being borne in mind that if a high standard is set seasonal variations will tend not to be judged significant even when they should be whereas if a low standard is set they will tend to be judged significant even when they should not be. In practice it is usual to set the level of significance arbitrarily at 5 per cent which means that a false scent will be followed on the average in only one out of twenty occasions.

The information required for carrying out this test is obtained by dividing the sum of squares of the observations into several independent parts, one associated with the mean value of the series, one associated with the deviations of seasonal means about the general mean and the other associated with the deviations of the actual observations about their respective seasonal means. This information is conveniently set out in the form of an analysis of variance as follows.

Analysis of Variance for Model (6.14) = (6.18)

VARIANCE	DEGREES OF FREEDOM	SUM OF SQUARES	
		SUFFIX NOTATION	MATRIX NOTATION
Mean value	1	$m\, n\, \bar{y}^2$	$y'[i(i'i)^{-1}\, i']y$
Between seasons	$m-1$	$n\sum_s (\bar{y}_s-\bar{y})^2$	$y'[S(S'S)^{-1}S'-i(i'i)^{-1}i']y$
Within seasons	$m(n-1)$	$\sum_s \sum_t (y_{st}-\bar{y}_s)^2$	$y'[I-S(S'S)^{-1}S']y$
Total	$m\, n$	$\sum_s \sum_t y^2_{st}$	$y'[I]y$

Mean squares (or variance estimates) corresponding to the sums of squares shown in the table are obtained by dividing the latter by their respective degrees of freedom. On the assumption that the ε_{st} are normally distributed, a test for the significance of the variance between seasons can be obtained from the ratio of the mean square between seasons to the mean square within seasons since, on the assumption that $\beta = 0$, this ratio, being the ratio of two independent estimates of the same population variance, has an F-distribution with $m-1$ and $m\,(n-1)$ degrees of freedom. This distribution is conveniently tabulated in a number of standard works on statistics such as the collection of tables prepared by Fisher and Yates [10].

In practice it is not very likely that the time series to be investigated will be trendless. If there is a trend in the series, the model (6.18) will not be appropriate because the means for seasons which occur later in the year will tend to be systematically higher (lower) than the means for those which occur earlier in the year on account of the upward (down-ward) trend. Accordingly the relative magnitude of these means will reflect the trend as well as the seasonal component in the variation of the series. They require to be adjusted therefore by reference to the average upward or downward movement of the series from one season to the next and this can be approximated by allowing for a linear trend in the series. With this addition the model takes the form

$$y = S\gamma + t\lambda + \varepsilon \tag{6.26}$$

where the vector t denotes the numbers $1, \ldots, mn$ each with the mean value of the series $(mn + 1)/2$, subtracted. In this case, the least-squares estimators c and l of γ and λ are

$$c = (S'S)^{-1} S' (y - tl) \tag{6.27}$$

and

$$l = (t'Mt)^{-1} t'My \tag{6.28}$$

where

$$M = [I - S(S'S)^{-1}S'] \tag{6.29}$$

Equation (6.27) shows that c is equal to the seasonal means of y after a linear residual trend has been extracted. It will be noticed, however, that the expression for c can be written in a way which is formally similar to the expression for l. Thus if

$$N = [I - t(t't)^{-1}t'] \tag{6.30}$$

then

$$c = (S'NS)^{-1}S'Ny \tag{6.31}$$

Model (6.26) may be expected to provide a reasonably satisfactory hypothesis in many practical cases. It does not, however, involve any consideration of the possibility that the seasonal pattern may be changing. This possibility ought clearly to be introduced into the analysis. The hypothesis of a uniform change in the seasonal pattern can readily be introduced by replacing the vector t by a matrix T where

$$T = \hat{t}S \tag{6.32}$$

so that T is related to t in a manner similar to that in which S is related to i. With this extension, the model takes the form

$$y = i\alpha + S\beta + t\lambda + T\mu + \varepsilon$$
$$= S(i_m\alpha + \beta) + T(i_m\lambda + \mu) + \varepsilon$$
$$= S\gamma + T\nu + \varepsilon \tag{6.33}$$

From (6.33) the least-squares estimators c and n of γ and ν can readily be written down. Once this is done the estimators a, b, l and m of α, β, λ and μ are obtained from the relationships

$$a = (i'_m i_m)^{-1} i'_m c \qquad (6.34)$$

$$b = c - i_m a \qquad (6.35)$$

$$l = (i'_m i_m)^{-1} i'_m n \qquad (6.36)$$

$$m = n - i_m l \qquad (6.37)$$

With this model it is possible to test whether the hypothesis of a constant seasonal pattern is justified by the observations. This is done by first testing whether the seasonal residual trends differ among themselves. If they do, there is evidence of a changing seasonal pattern. The series should then be adjusted not for a constant but for a uniformly changing difference between seasons though it must be recognised that such a form of seasonal variation with constant coefficients can hardly persist indefinitely. If the seasonal residual trends do not differ significantly it is next possible to test whether a significant part of the variation left after a general mean and trend have been extracted from the series can be accounted for by fitting a set of seasonal means. If it can then there is evidence of a constant seasonal pattern and the series should be adjusted accordingly. If it cannot then there is no evidence of systematic seasonal effects such as can be represented by a linear model.

The analysis involved in carrying out these tests is more complicated than the simple analysis of variance so far considered. In this case there are two variables y and t which are being classified by season and the partitioning of the sum of squares, $y'y$, takes the form of an analysis of covariance as set out, for example, by Kendall [13, pp. 237-40]. Adapted to the present problem it can be formulated as follows:

Analysis of Covariance for Model (6.33)

VARIANCE	DEGREES OF FREEDOM	SUM OF SQUARES
1. General mean	1	$y'[i(i'i)^{-1}i']y$
2. General trend	1	$y'[t(t't)^{-1}t']y$
3. Between seasonal means	$m-1$	$y'[S(S'S)^{-1}S' + Mt\,(t'Mt)^{-1}t'M - i(i'i)^{-1}i' - t(t't)^{-1}t']y$
4. Between seasonal trends	$m-1$	$y'[MT(T'MT)^{-1}T'M - Mt(t'Mt)^{-1}t'M]y$
5. Residual	$m(n-2)$	$y'[I - S(S'S)^{-1}S' - MT(T'MT)^{-1}T'M]y$
6. Total	mn	$y'[I]y$

The first question to be disposed of is whether there is evidence of a uniformly changing seasonal pattern. This is done by testing the significance of the difference between seasonal residual trends. On the usual assumptions the variance ratio obtained from rows 4 and 5 of the table has the F-distribution with the degrees of freedom shown. If the hypothesis of different seasonal residual trends is rejected, the sums of squares and degrees of freedom shown in rows 4 and 5 are added together and provide the information for a new estimate of the residual variance with which to compare the variance attributable to differences between seasonal means as shown in row 3. If the hypothesis of a difference between seasonal means (apart from trend effects) is sustained then adjustment for a constant seasonal pattern, given by the elements of b, should be made. If the hypothesis is rejected no adjustment can properly be made. In terms of the present model the series can at best be expressed in terms of a general mean and a general trend which apply to all the observations. It will be noticed that if the hypothesis of a difference between seasonal trends is rejected model (6.33) reduces to model (6.26).

The object of the process which has just been described is to put any series analysed into one of three categories which depend on whether some adjustment or no adjustment should be made for seasonal variations and in the former case whether the adjustment should be constant or changing. Many complications can be introduced into this procedure but before considering these an example will be given of an application of the method.

4. AN APPLICATION OF THE METHOD

The foregoing procedure will now be illustrated by reference to a quarterly series of the volume of consumers' expenditure in the United Kingdom which is available since the first quarter of 1948. Model (6.33) was applied to the twenty-eight quarterly observations from the beginning of 1948 through 1954. Since, in general, it seems reasonable to suppose that a seasonal pattern can better be expressed in relative than in absolute terms, the common logarithms of the series rather than the actual values were used in the analysis.

The original series was expressed in £ billion (10^9), of 1948 purchasing power and the estimates of the parameters are as follows:

$$a = \quad 0.3585 \qquad\qquad (6.38)$$

$$b = \begin{bmatrix} -0.0270 \\ -0.0047 \\ 0.0095 \\ 0.0222 \end{bmatrix} \qquad\qquad (6.39)$$

$$l = \quad 0.00142 \qquad\qquad (6.40)$$

83

and

$$m = \begin{bmatrix} -0.00002 \\ -0.00022 \\ -0.00029 \\ 0.00053 \end{bmatrix} \qquad (6.41)$$

The data for the analysis of covariance can be set out as follows:

VARIANCE	DEGREES OF FREEDOM	SUM OF SQUARES	MEAN SQUARE
1. General mean	1	3.211553	...
2. General trend	1	0.005460	...
3. Between seasons	3	0.009346	0.0031153
4. Between trends	3	0.000185	0.0000617
5. Residual	20	0.002475	0.0001238
6. Total	28	3.229022	...

The ratio of the mean squares shown in rows 4 and 5 is less than unity and, accordingly, the null hypothesis, that there is no difference between the seasonal trends, is sustained. The mean square for rows 4 and 5 together is 0.0001157 and the ratio of the mean square in row 3 to this value is 26.9. This value is definitely significant.

In this case therefore there is evidence of a constant seasonal pattern given by the elements of the vector b. The multipliers to be applied to the different seasons of the actual series are obtained by reversing the signs of these elements and taking antilogarithms. These multipliers, taken in order through the seasons, are on the basis of model (6.33): 1.064, 1.011, 0.978 and 0.950.

In this example the analysis of covariance has shown that the variables which are in model (6.33) but not in model (6.26) do not make a significant contribution to the variance. It does not follow from this, however, that (6.26) is to be preferred to (6.33) and this would only be the case if the elements of m were, on the whole, less than their standard errors. If model (6.26) were applied in the present example the elements of b would be: —0.0271, —0.0048, 0.0092 and 0.0227. For this model, therefore, the multipliers are: 1.064, 1.011, 0.979 and 0.949. The differences between these values and those given in the preceding paragraph are negligible.

The adjusted und unadjusted series for the 28 quarters used in the analysis are as follows. The adjustments are based on model (6.33).

It will be noted that, as is to be expected with relative adjusters, the adjusted totals are slightly different from the unadjusted totals.

TABLE 4. CONSUMERS' EXPENDITURE IN THE UNITED KINGDOM

£ (1948) billion.

		1948	1949	1950	1951	1952	1953	1954
Unadjusted	I	1.943	1.973	2.022	2.136	2.012	2.067	2.128
	II	2.086	2.132	2.139	2.150	2.096	2.202	2.277
	III	2.176	2.197	2.257	2.166	2.191	2.269	2.370
	IV	2.191	2.268	2.324	2.218	2.279	2.381	2.523
Total	....	8.396	8.570	8.742	8.670	8.578	8.919	9.298
Adjusted	I	2.068	2.099	2.152	2.273	2.141	2.199	2.265
	II	2.109	2.155	2.162	2.173	2.119	2.226	2.302
	III	2.129	2.149	2.208	2.119	2.143	2.220	2.319
	IV	2.082	2.155	2.208	2.108	2.165	2.263	2.397
Total	....	8.388	8.558	8.731	8.673	8.568	8.908	9.283

5. EXTENSIONS AND DEVELOPMENTS

The type of model described in section 3 is extremely simple and for a variety of reasons it may be necessary to introduce further refinements and complications.

In the first place it will frequently be desirable to consider the possible significance of specific influences. Thus it may be important to decide whether the varying dates of Easter or Whitsun or abnormalities in rainfall or temperature exert a significant influence on the series. This can be done by introducing into the analysis variables which correspond to these different factors in a form which ensures that they are independent of S and T. If F^* denotes a matrix the columns of which contain the values of a particular factor over the period of observation, then the component, F say, of F^* orthogonal to S and T is

$$F = [I - S(S'S)^{-1}S' - MT(T'MT)^{-1}T'M] F^* \qquad (6.42)$$

Thus, for example, if F^*_1 denotes a column of F^* introduced to test whether there is a significant variation associated with the presence of Easter then the elements of F^*_1 will be unity in any season which actually contains Easter and otherwise zero. In a similar way rainfall can be introduced by including in F^* a column, F^*_2 say, which represents observations on rainfall. If, as will sometimes be the case, rainfall has to be introduced in such a way that it can have a different influence in each season then the column F^*_2 must be replaced by m columns each of which shows the rainfall level in a particular season and contains zeros in all other seasons.

Since F is orthogonal to S and T its introduction into the model will remove a part to the original residual variance. It is thus possible to test whether the influences contained in F contribute significantly to the total variance in addition to the contribution made by S and T which is not allocated to specific factors.

In the second place it seems likely that in many cases it will not be plausible to assume that the true residual is independently distributed with constant variance. In such cases the method of least squares will not lead to estimators of minimum variance. The solution of the problem posed by this state of affairs would be extremely difficult but it seems likely, on the basis of experience, that the original hypothesis of independence will be more plausible if it is made in respect of season to season changes. Thus if z denotes the first differences of y, then (6.33) is replaced by

$$z = S\gamma + T\nu + \varepsilon \qquad (6.43)$$

The estimation of the parameters γ and ν in (6.43) is exactly the same as in (6.33) but the significance test takes a slightly different form and indeed is somewhat simpler. The analysis of covariance may be carried out on the following basis.

Analysis of Covariance for Model (6.43)

VARIANCE	DEGREES OF FREEDOM	SUM OF SQUARES
1. General mean	1	$z'[i(i'i)^{-1}i']z$
2. Between seasonal means	$m-1$	$z'[S(S'S)^{-1}S'-i(i'i)^{-1}i']z$
3. Trends	m	$z'[MT(T'MT)^{-1}T'M]z$
4. Residual	$m(n-2)$	$z'[I-S(S'S)^{-1}S'-MT(T'MT)^{-1}T'M]z$
5. Total	mn	$z'[I]z$

The terminology used in this formulation is appropriate to first differences but needs some reinterpretation in terms of original series. A non-zero mean in first differences implies a linear trend in the original series. The deviations of the seasonal means from the general mean after allowance for residual trends provide estimates of the season to season differences in the constant seasonal pattern. Any residual trends in the system are associated with the variable MT. Accordingly the mean squares of rows 3 and 4 may be compared to test if there is a changing seasonal pattern in the original series. If this hypothesis is rejected the mean squares of row 2 and rows 3 and 4 combined may be compared to test whether there is a constant seasonal pattern in the original series.

If model (6.43) is applied to the series of consumers' expenditures from the change between the last quarter of 1948 and the first quarter of 1949 to the change between the last two quarters of 1954, the results are as follows.

$$a = \quad 0.002286 \qquad\qquad (6.44)$$

$$b = \begin{bmatrix} -0.046537 \\ 0.020324 \\ 0.012541 \\ 0.013673 \end{bmatrix} \qquad (6.45)$$

$$l = \quad 0.000193 \qquad\qquad (6.46)$$

$$m = \begin{bmatrix} -0.000193 \\ -0.000173 \\ -0.000146 \\ 0.000512 \end{bmatrix} \qquad (6.47)$$

The analysis of variance in this case confirms the earlier conclusion. Estimates of the elements of b appropriate to the original series are obtained by accumulating the elements of b in (6.45), advancing the resulting numbers by one season, so that the value for season IV is zero, and subtracting the mean of the accumulated series from each seasonal value. The resulting numbers are: —0.0249, —0.0046, 0.0079 and 0.0216 which are hardly distinguishable from the values given in (6.39). The multipliers in this case are: 1.059, 1.011, 0.982 and 0.951.

In the third place, it may be objected that a linear model is unlikely to give a sufficiently realistic treatment of the trend of the series and that it would be preferable to analyse the deviations about a moving average rather than about a linear trend. There is no difficulty in reformulating the model so as to take account of this objection since all that need be done is to substitute deviations from a moving average trend for the original observations.

A moving average model was constructed with the consumers' expenditure data by subtracting from log y a two-quarters moving average of a four-quarters moving average of log y. The series so constructed covered the six years from the third quarter of 1948 through the second quarter of 1954. The values obtained for the elements of b are: —0.0251, —0.0044, 0.0087 and 0.0208. The multipliers obtained from these estimates, namely 1.060, 1.010, 0.980 and 0.953, are hardly different from those obtained earlier.

6. THE COMBINATION OF SEASONAL CHAINS

The preceding sections have been concerned with adjustments for seasonal variation. Formally similar adjustments can be used for an entirely different purpose, namely for combining a set of seasonal chains into a single series which runs through all the seasons. This problem can be described as follows. Regular economic information is frequently collected for each season in the form of the percentage change in this season over the same season a year ago. If the level of each season in a particular year is put equal to unity then a series can be constructed for each season by multiplying out the percentage changes. These separate series are not directly comparable but they can be made so by an application of the technique described in this chapter. If the separate series are adjusted in this way there will result a series, necessarily free of normal seasonal variation, which runs continuously through the seasons.

VII

THE TREATMENT
OF NON-COMMODITY FLOWS

1. THE TREATMENT OF AGGREGATES WHICH ARE NOT ENTIRELY COMPOSED OF COMMODITY FLOWS

The discussion so far has been concentrated on the problems, arising in the construction of index-numbers, which involve only the treatment of commodity flows and aggregates. In terms of table 1 the flows of this kind into and out of the production accounts were rearranged into two sets, values added and final expenditures, each of which sums to total domestic product. Being commodity flows, each of the component transactions can in principle be regarded as the product of a price and a quantity and it is from these components that the price and quantity index-numbers are constructed.

By these means, various aspects of which have been discussed in detail in earlier sections of this Report, it is in principle possible to express any commodity flow in terms of constant prices. It is clear, however, that many of the transactions recorded in a system of social accounts do not represent commodity flows and cannot be thought of as the sum of prices times quantities. Obvious examples are the current transfers from general government to the private sector. Thus, for example, the payment of a weekly sickness benefit cannot in any meaningful sense be regarded as the purchase of so much of some commodity at such and such a price per unit but only as the payment of a certain sum designed to relieve the immediate financial difficulties which the recipient is likely to be in as a consequence of sickness. The change in the real value of sickness benefits has to do, in ordinary speech, with the change in real consumption that is made possible for the recipient and not with the output of some notional industry devoted to the relief of distress consequent on sickness.

Thus the reduction of non-commodity flows to terms of constant prices involves a different kind of operation to that required for commodity flows. Since in the nature of the case there is no accompanying commodity flow which might be expressed in terms of quantity and price it is necessary to adopt a different point of view and to consider the various uses to which the purely monetary flow might be put.

The distinction that has just been made is important because non-commodity flows are important in the national accounts and a measure of them in terms of constant prices is frequently required. Thus, for example, personal income and personal saving fall into the class of aggregates of non-commodity transactions and so do national totals of income and product. The search for deflators of these totals is essentially the search for appropriate collections of commodities on which these sums of money might be spent and in relation to the changing cost of which they can, in an interesting way, be expressed in real terms.

2. THE ARBITRARY NATURE OF ATTEMPTS TO BALANCE AN ACCOUNTING SYSTEM IN REAL TERMS

There are innumerable possibilities in the choice of collections of commodities the price index-numbers for which may be used to express a series given in current money values in terms of constant purchasing power. It might be supposed that the choice of suitable price series for non-commodity flows could be made by combining the price series for commodity flows with the requirement that the complete accounting system, as set out for example in table 1, should balance, period by period, in real as well as in money terms. The restriction on the choice of price series which this procedure would imply would be arbitrary, though perhaps convenient, but it might be supposed that at least it would provide a unique solution of the problem. It will be shown in this section that the solution obtained is not only arbitrary from an economic point of view but also, except in simplified cases, depends on one or more parameters which may be fixed arbitrarily.

The required price index-numbers may be regarded as unknowns to be chosen in such a way that the accounting constraints of the system remain satisfied when it is expressed in terms of constant prices. If there are n unknown price index-numbers and $N + 1$ accounts in the system then the n index-numbers are to be so determined that the N independent constraints (or equations) are satisfied.

It can be seen that if $n < N$ it is, in general, impossible that the individual accounts should balance in real terms. This can be illustrated by the case of a simple closed economy in which there is one consolidated production account and one consolidated non-production account. The former receives from the latter the proceeds of all expenditures in the system on commodities, E, and pays out to the latter all incomes earned in the course of productive activity, Y. Thus the accounting structure is as follows:

	CONSOLIDATED PRODUCTION ACCOUNT	ALL OTHER ACCOUNTS CONSOLIDATED
Consolidated production account	—	E
All other accounts consolidated	Y	—

90

It is clear that if factor services can be treated as commodities so that the change in Y in real terms represents the average change in the quantity of factor inputs into the economy then this change will only be equal to the independently estimated change in E in real terms if the average change in the productivity of the factors of production is zero. In this case $N = 1$ and $n = 0$ and there is no means of forcing an equality between the changes in real terms of E and Y by choosing an appropriate price index for one of them because both price index-numbers are independently calculated.

If, as in this Report, E is and Y is not regarded as an aggregate of commodity transactions, then the two consolidated accounts can be made to balance in real terms by dividing the change in Y ($=$ the change in E) expressed in current money terms by the price index appropriate to E. In this case $N = n = 1$ and the requirement that the two accounts must remain balanced in real terms permits a unique measure of the real change in Y to be determined.

A slightly more complicated case arises if the consolidated non-production account is divided into an appropriation account and a capital transactions account. In this case E is divided into two parts, current expenditure of commodities, C, and asset formation, I. The amount $Y - C = S$ represents saving and is a non-commodity transaction between the appropriation and capital transactions accounts. The accounting structure is as follows:

	PRODUCTION ACCOUNT	APPROPRIATION ACCOUNT	CAPITAL TRANSACTIONS ACCOUNT
Production account	—	C	I
Appropriation account	Y	—	—
Capital transactions account ...	—	S	—

In this case Y and S are non-commodity transactions and so $N = n = 2$. It is possible to express these transactions in real terms so as to maintain the accounts in balance. To achieve this end the change in Y must be adjusted by the price change appropriate to the commodity transactions $C + I$ and the change in S must be adjusted by the price change appropriate to I. If the change in S were adjusted by the price change appropriate to C the production account would balance in real terms but the other two accounts would not. If the changes in S and in Y were adjusted by the price change appropriate to C then the appropriation account would balance in real terms but the other two accounts would not.

The last case to be considered is a further extension of the simple accounting model so that it can represent an open economy. This can be done by adding a consolidated external account to the three given in

91

the last example. It may be assumed to begin with that there are three entries in this account, namely: X = exports, M = imports and $L = X - M$ = net lending. The accounting structure is now as follows :

	PRODUCTION ACCOUNT	APPRO-PRIATION ACCOUNT	CAPITAL TRANS-ACTIONS ACCOUNT	EXTERNAL ACCOUNT
Production account	—	C	I	X
Appropriation account	Y	—	—	—
Capital transactions account	—	S	—	—
External account	M	—	L	—

In this case Y, S and L are non-commodity transactions and so $N = n = 3$. It is again possible to find price-indices with which to adjust the changes in Y, S and L so that the four accounts invariably balance in real terms. The appropriate price index-numbers are given by the equations

$$Y = C + I + X - M \qquad (7.1)$$

$$L = X - M \qquad (7.2)$$

$$S = Y - C = I + L = I + X - M \qquad (7.3)$$

The terms on the right-hand side of these equations represent aggregates of commodity transactions and accordingly to maintain the balance of the accounts in real terms it is necessary for Y, L and S to be adjusted by the price index-numbers appropriate to $(C + I + X - M)$, $(X - M)$ and $(I + X - M)$ respectively.

Suppose now that the rest of the world makes investment income payments, V, to the economy under discussion. This transaction which is not in commodities will appear at the intersection of the column for the external account and the row for the appropriation account. In this case $N = 3$ and $n = 4$. The three accounting constraints are still sufficient to determine a unique price index-number for Y but they are no longer sufficient to determine unique price index-numbers for S and L or for V. Instead an infinite set of price index-numbers can be found for S, L and V which depend on an arbitrary parameter.

If equations similar to (7.1) to (7.3) are written down for this accounting structure it is found that the equation for Y is still that shown in (7.1) so that Y can still be expressed in terms of commodity transactions. This cannot be done, however, for S, L and V and examination will show that only their differences by pairs can be so expressed. Thus

$$S - L = Y - C + M - X = I \qquad (7.4)$$

$$V - L = M - X \qquad (7.5)$$

$$S - V = Y - C = I + X - M \qquad (7.6)$$

Suppose that the above symbols denote deflated values and further assume that $L = L'$, a known series. Then

$$S = Y - C + M - X + L' = I + L' \qquad (7.7)$$

and

$$V = M - X + L' \qquad (7.8)$$

If the successive values of L' are fixed arbitrarily (7.7) and (7.8) provide deflated values for S and V such that the accounting structure invariably balances after adjustment to constant prices.

Reflection shows that the problem just described is formally identical to that of indirect estimation of the elements in an accounting system by the method of residuals. It is possible to determine residually the value of at most N transactions in a system of $N + 1$ accounts. If the accounts are represented graphically by points and if the unknowns, the values of which are to be determined residually, are represented by branches connecting these points, then the values of all unknowns can be determined simultaneously provided that there are no loops (or closed circuits) in the diagram. If all the points are connected in a single network (without loops) then it is just possible to determine the values of the unknowns by using all the accounting constraints. If the points are grouped together in two or more unconnected networks (each without a loop) then all the values of the unknowns can be determined from the accounting constraints but not all the constraints have to be used. If on the other hand there is a loop in the diagram then the values of the unknowns which form part of the loop cannot be determined uniquely but all are dependent on a single arbitrary parameter. If an unknown forms a part of k loops then it may take a multiply infinite number of values, the multiplicity being equal to k.

The conclusion of this section is that, in general, it is impossible to find a unique set of deflated values of the non-commodity transactions in an accounting system such that the accounts continue to balance in real terms. In certain simplified cases the deflated values obtained are unique but at the same time they may not be appropriate for all purposes. Thus in the second example above it was necessary to deflate saving by the price index appropriate to asset formation and in the third it was necessary to deflate net lending abroad by the difference between export and import prices weighted respectively by the value of exports and imports in the base period.

3. VARIOUS MEASURES OF THE NATIONAL INCOME AT CONSTANT PRICES

There are several quite different ways in which an attempt might be made to express a series of the money national income in terms of constant prices. The resulting estimates would, in general, be quite different from one another.

1. If it were possible to measure the quantity of the inputs of the different factors of production into productive processes the national income could be treated as a commodity total in its own right. A quantity measure could be constructed which would represent the real input (net) of the different kinds of factor supplied by the economy under investigation into the world economy. For labour it might be possible to construct a measure of real input, but it is not clear how this could be done for other factors of production.

If a quantity measure were to be constructed on these lines its movements would not, in general, be the same as those of the domestic product even in the case of a closed economy. The reason is that over time the productivity of the factors of production would be likely to change. If productivity were increasing the domestic product at constant prices would rise through time relative to the domestic input at constant prices. The former divided by the latter would provide a measure of the average increase in productivity of the factors of production.

2. Real income might, for a closed economy, be defined equal to real product. This means that the quantity index for the domestic product is used again for the corresponding income concept.

If, however, the economy is open this procedure does not provide a complete solution. In the first place it may be assumed that there is a certain amount of net factor income from or to abroad and this is not a commodity transaction. The usual procedure is to reduce this net factor income from abroad to constant prices by means of an index of import prices on the ground that the use of such income from a national point of view is to finance a certain amount of imports. Apart from the practical point that index-numbers of import prices usually refer only to visible trade it can be seen that net income from abroad could equally well be used either to reduce exports or to obtain financial claims on other countries. If it is used for the latter purpose there is no obvious means of expressing it in terms of constant prices while if it is used to reduce exports its contribution to real income will differ from that obtained from the assumption that it is used to increase imports if the movement of export prices differs from the movement of import prices.

Apart from the question of the real value of income from overseas investment there is the question of the real value of imports and exports. Thus it may be said that exports, like income from overseas investment, are useful to a country because they finance the purchase of imports. From this point of view the quantity of exports is irrelevant to real income; what is important is the quantity of imports that can be bought with the proceeds of the exports.

If this line of thought is accepted it would seem appropriate to deflate the value of exports by means of the import (not export) price index. Since the value of imports adjusted by this index has in any case to be deducted in reducing final expenditures to constant prices, national income at constant prices is given by the sum of the current and capital expenditure on commodities at constant prices by the households, government and enterprises of the economy and the excess of exports and net income from abroad over imports divided by import prices.

There is no obvious justification for making this assumption since the export surplus is not in fact used to purchase imports at the time at which it arises and in the future it may be used to purchase home-produced goods by means of a reduction in future exports. Thus while it seems reasonable to adjust for the terms of trade as above if the value of imports and exports are always in balance and there are not other elements in the balance of payments it does not appear that this procedure is equally satisfactory in the general case.

3. It might be supposed that appropriate deflators for non-commodity flows could be obtained by combining the deflators for commodity flows with the requirement that each account of the system should balance when its entries are expressed in terms of constant prices. In the preceding section it was shown that in certain simplified cases this is indeed formally possible although the results obtainable by this method are of doubtful economic significance. In the general case, however, unique deflators for the non-commodity flows cannot be obtained by this method.

4. In view of the difficulties and shortcomings of the possibilities so far examined it seems best to accept the fact that a non-commodity flow can only be expressed in terms of constant prices with respect to a bill of commodities given independently. If this view is accepted it would seem that the most appropriate bill of commodities is given by the final purchases of the economy in a given period. These purchases comprise the current and capital purchases of all sectors and are equal to the sum of private purchases for consumption, general government purchases for consumption and domestic asset formation. If the gross national product is deflated by the price index appropriate to this commodity total its movements over time will show its purchasing power over the collection of commodities which entered into these purchases in a given period.

4. ALTERNATIVE CONCEPTS OF NON-COMMODITY FLOWS AT CONSTANT PRICES

Social accounting data are of fundamental importance in all forms of aggregative econometric model-building and it is generally agreed that for this purpose the social accounts should, as far as possible, be compiled on a consistent basis in both money and real terms and that discrepancies and residual errors should be removed by a suitable system of adjustment. It has been seen that while the commodity flows in a social accounting system can in principle be reduced to constant prices in a consistent manner the attempt to do the same for non-commodity flows leads to a fundamental form of arbitrariness. For a given purpose, however, it may not be difficult to decide on an appropriate price series to serve as a deflator. Thus, for example, it may be satisfactory for many purposes to deflate personal saving by means of a price index of consumers' goods and services since these are the commodities on which consumers' disposable incomes would have been spent if they had not been saved and it would seem useful therefore to express money saving in terms of its purchasing power over this alternative. In a social accounting system, however, saving will also appear as an incoming flow into the capital transactions account and from the investors' point of view it may seem more appropriate to deflate saving by means of the price index for domestic asset formation since usually the greater part of saving will be devoted to this object. If this is done there will be two measures of saving in real terms, one of which is more or less appropriate to savers while the other is more or less appropriate to investors. If the prices of consumption goods have risen more (or less) than the prices of capital goods then on this basis the supply of saving in real terms will have risen less (more) than the demand. It has been suggested by Carl Christ that discrepancies of this kind may be significant in model-building and that consideration should be given to the development of social accounts in which such alternative measures appear. No attempt will be made here to develop this suggestion.

VIII

GENERAL PROBLEMS OF MEASUREMENT

1. INTRODUCTION

The problems to be taken up in this chapter relate to the methods to be followed in making the actual measurements. The most important problem is almost certainly the selection of the price and quantity indicators and this is considered in section 2. It is followed in section 3 by a discussion of alternative indicators of prices and quantities. In section 4 attention is turned to the question of short-period indicators and this is followed in section 5 by a discussion of the problem of weighting. Section 6 contains some brief remarks on the choice of a base period.

2. THE SELECTION OF INDICATORS

The term indicator is used throughout this Report to mean an individual price or quantity series and the term index-number (or index) is used to mean a weighted average of the changes in individual indicators. In most cases the index is reached as a result of combining the indicators and so the latter cannot be chosen by reference to their ability to reproduce the desired index. An exception to this statement might arise if it were desired to interpolate on, say, a monthly basis an annual index of production or prices based on successive annual censuses. In this case it might be worthwhile to consider the relationship between the annual index and the available monthly indicators and to select and weight the indicators by references to their relationships with the index. Further, if in these circumstances there arose the question of extending the collection of monthly indicators it might be worthwhile to devise a sampling scheme based on the relationships between the corresponding annual indicators and the annual index.

In this Report discussion is confined to the more usual approach in which certain weights, the general nature of which has already been described, are associated with different industries or different commodities and in which suitable indicators are found which are to be combined with these weights. The selection of indicators will as a rule be largely determined by the kind of information available but in using this to the best advantage and in supplementing it efficiently certain general principles should be borne in mind. The discussion here follows the treatment given in [3].

In the first place, each value unit of net output or final product should receive the same attention whether it forms a small part of a large industry or final product group or the whole of a small one. In practical work there is an almost inevitable tendency to attempt to obtain indicators for every item and it may easily come about that more time is spent in trying to obtain an indicator for a small item than in improving the indicator for a large item although the changes that might be made in the latter would almost certainly have far more effect on the index than the inclusion or exclusion of the former. Thus, for example, it is usually possible to obtain an indicator of beer consumed which may be expressed either in bulk barrels, which is a measure of liquid volume, or in standard barrels, which is a measure of alcohol volume. This latter does and the former does not allow for variations in the strength of the beer which is known to be an important element in its quality. It may be hurriedly decided to adopt one or other of these measures either because the matter is not carefully considered or because in the past the two have moved closely together. They may not however continue to move closely together and, if beer consumption is a large item, the choice of indicator may have a much larger effect on the index than the inclusion or exclusion of an indicator for a negligible item such as mead or herb wine. Another example would be the possible desirability of obtaining information on the production of coal by grades before searching for an indicator for manufactured fuel.

Similar situations may easily arise in the construction of output index-numbers especially where by-products are involved. For economic reasons it may have been usual in the past to produce a main product and its by-product in fixed proportions in which case it may seem sufficient to carry the whole weight of this production on an indicator for the main product. If however this proportion is changed the resulting index may move differently from one based on indicators for both products. The effect of this will be serious if the by-product carries a large weight.

In the second place, the fact that all errors cannot be corrected is not a valid reason for failing to correct some of them. One of the more obvious applications of this principle relates to quality changes for some but not all of which corrections can usually be made. Since there is no reason to suppose that quality corrections will offset each other it follows that the index will be improved if as many as possible of these corrections are made.

In the third place, it is useless to reject indicators because they are not perfect unless there is something better that can be put in their place. Thus employment may be a bad indicator of output in a particular trade but it may be better to use it than to assume that the output of the trade moves with the output of other trades in the same industry or with the index of output as a whole. If the employment indicator is not used then either the coverage of the index must be more narrowly defined or the weight of the trade must be carried by the indicators for other trades.

3. ALTERNATIVE INDICATORS OF PRICES AND QUANTITIES

If it may be assumed, as will frequently be the case, that value series are available for the groups of net outputs and final expenditures for which quantity and price index-numbers are required, then a current-weighted price or quantity index can readily be obtained indirectly by calculating respectively a base-weighted quantity or price index. Indeed if it is not proposed to calculate directly index-numbers of both quantities and prices then, if all the necessary value figures are available, it is possible to combine the calculation of price index-numbers for some groups with quantity index-numbers for others. For consistency, the price index-numbers should be current-weighted if the quantity index-numbers are base-weighted and vice-versa though, if the weights appropriate to the two periods are such that L is approximately equal to P then the inconsistency due to combining directly estimated base-weighted quantity index-numbers with indirectly estimated current-weighted quantity index-numbers is unlikely to be large.

The respective characteristics of good quantity and price indicators are somewhat different. In the case of quantity indicators it is important to obtain as complete a coverage as possible in each series used. For the movements in the quantities of different commodities, even if they are made by the same industry and involve much the same processes, may differ widely and the same is true of the movements of production of a given commodity by different firms or of consumption by different classes of consumer. On the other hand, there are usually a wide variety of possible types of quantity indicator which, while not ideal, approach, according to circumstances, more or less closely to the ideal.

The situation with price indicators is different. In practice there are very few substitutes for a knowledge of actual price movements but it is not so important to obtain the completeness of coverage that is desirable with quantity indicators. Prices charged for close substitutes by different firms or in different parts of a country are likely, in many cases, to show similar movements even if their absolute level is a little different. The same is true for commodities which are made from similar raw materials by similar processes. Thus it is possible to apply sampling procedures to the construction of price indices for the varieties of a product or for related products on a scale altogether greater than is appropriate for the corresponding quantities.

In the following discussion of alternative indicators, quantity indicators for net outputs and for final expenditures are considered separately and price indicators are discussed briefly at the end of the section.

Net output quantity indicators. It can readily be seen that the problem of finding indicators is enormously simplified if it can be assumed that commodity inputs into industries are proportional to commodity outputs. For in this case a single indicator either of gross output or of any one commodity input will provide an indicator of the net output of an industry. This far-reaching assumption is made in most actual index-numbers of production without as a rule any test of its validity. It is the same assumption as that which is made in input-output models with fixed production coefficients. Every effort should be made to check this assumption although in practice it may be difficult to do this except where it does not have to be made. Thus, if a country has an annual census of production with details of at least the main material inputs into each industry it is possible to check whether or not these material inputs vary in proportion to output. If they do not however it is possible to make the more elaborate calculation required. If this information is not available it might nevertheless be possible to gain an impression of the validity of the assumption of proportionality in different industries on the basis of trade or technical information or of the experience of other countries. An interesting study of this subject relating to manufacturing industries in Canada has appeared in [8].

If the above assumption can be made, then any of a number of indicators can be used for the movement of net output. If the assumption cannot be made then alternative indicators can be used in place of outputs or inputs respectively. The following may be mentioned:

1. Total outputs of the industry. This is the sum of all quantities sold to different buyers adjusted for stock changes and is the proper indicator for gross output. If more than one commodity is sold by an industry the weight for each commodity is its total selling value less the estimated profit on the net transfers to stock.

2. Total sales by the industry. This indicator differs conceptually from (1) by the amount of the change in stocks. Its use implies, therefore, that this stock change is ignored.

3. Deliveries by the industry. This indicator fails to take account of stock changes and may also involve a time-lag as compared with sales. In many cases this lag may be of minor importance.

4. Input of materials. There will usually be many of these and their weighted sum is the proper index of input.

5. Materials purchased. This indicator differs from the preceding one by the change in the stocks of materials held.

6. Employment or man-hours (labour input). This indicator requires to be adjusted for any changes in the productivity of labour input. Even if this cannot be done, or can be done only roughly, it may be better to use this indicator than to assume that the net output to which it corresponds varies with some other net output.

7. Values (of output, etc.) adjusted for price changes. This indicator may be useful in cases where, for one reason or another, it is impracticable to measure quantities directly. The reason for this may be that the constituent commodities cannot easily be classified into homogeneous groups or that, though the commodities are capable of being classified in this way, the resulting groups are exceedingly numerous or that information is in fact available about the movements of total value but not about the movements of the corresponding quantities.

8. Activity. Indicators of this kind may be useful if there is no other indicator of net output, being technically linked with the process

of production or connected with the requirement for the output of the industry. An example of a process indicator is the number of spindles or spindle-hours in operation in textiles. Possible requirement indicators are: the length of telephone wire as an indicator of amount of repair work being done on the telephone system; private car licences current as an indicator of the depreciation of roads by private users; the output of the building industry and agriculture as an indicator of consumption, and so indirectly of production, of handtools; the number of deaths as an indicator for the undertaking trade or for the production of tombstones.

Final expenditure quantity indicators.   In this sense final expenditures consist in current purchases of commodities by private consumers and general government, asset formation (fixed assets and stocks) and exports less imports.   As has already been explained the commodities which enter into the current purchases of private consumers are those which are received by the household (or other buying unit) and no attention is paid to any further transformation they may undergo within the household.   For general government a similar treatment should be adopted.

If these different classes of final sales are to be distinguished then the corresponding division of the flow of goods available must be made. Apart from this division, the flows being measured are the same as the gross output flows of the final goods industries and in most cases the indicators will be similar if not identical.   The following indicators may be mentioned:

1.   Quantities sold to the consumers.   Provided that quality changes are adequately reflected this series is a proper indicator.   Changes in producers' stocks must be included in an index of final expenditure as a whole since they form part of asset formation.

2.   Quantities delivered to retailers.   This indicator will provide a good approximation provided that there have not been large changes in retail stocks.

3.   Quantities withdrawn from bond.   This indicator is similar to (2).   It may be expected to work well for a commodity like beer where stock changes can hardly be large but may, on occasion, work badly for commodities like wine and spirits.   Thus there may be large withdrawals from bond in anticipation of budget changes in rates of duty with a corresponding fall in withdrawals after the budget.   Such changes will distort monthly or even quarterly figures though they may not be of much importance with annual figures.

4.   Output adjusted for imports and exports.   It may be necessary to use indicators of this kind.   They can be improved if it is possible to allow for stock changes and wastage.   If the commodity under consideration is not wholly used for consumption, it will be necessary to allocate supplies between consumers and other users.   The systematic use of all available information is greatly assisted if a supplies and disposals table is constructed for each commodity, the final use of which

is to be estimated by this method. The object of such a table is to account for total supplies from home production and imports in terms of industrial uses, wastage, stock change, exports and final purchases at home.

5. Labour input. It will usually be necessary to use this indicator for all personal services, and it will also play a large part in the measurement of government services since, in many cases, labour is the most important input into these.

6. Values (of sales, etc.) adjusted for price changes. This type of indicator will frequently be useful.

Price indicators. As already mentioned it is difficult to find alternatives to actual price movements. The one which readily suggests itself is an indirect measure obtained by dividing values by the corresponding quantities. The result of this calculation is usually termed average value. Such an indicator is likely to be unsatisfactory because it is generally necessary only when the corresponding quantity indicator is extremely crude so that changes in quality or in product composition are not properly reflected. An example of such an indicator arises in exports of such commodity groups as machinery where values and quantities measured in tons are often available. The replacement of a crude measure of this kind involves a considerable knowledge of the details of machinery exports and their prices and is likely to give rise to many problems of quality changes and of the appearance of new products.

In principle it would be possible to build up retail prices or wholesale prices from the other taken together with information on distributive margins. In practice this method is unlikely to give good results since it implies a detailed knowledge of the changes in the margins at each stage in the circulation of goods and, though this is usually of less importance, in the channels of trade themselves. Such knowledge is not usually available.

Finally, there are certain classes of commodity such as building repairs and much other construction work which do not lend themselves very readily to quantity estimation because it is hard to find a common quantity unit for the different pieces of work done. In such cases the best approach is probably to construct price series for typical pieces of repair or other work and to combine these to give a price indicator for repair work in general. If value figures of the work are available a measure of quantity can then be derived indirectly.

4. SHORT-PERIOD INDICATORS

If index-numbers are to be compiled for periods shorter than a year consideration must be given to the definition of these periods and their relationship to available information. Suppose that quantity index-numbers are being compiled for monthly periods, that is to say that it is desired to compare months. Several possibilities are now open.

The quantity indicators could relate (i) to the actual amounts produced in each month or (ii) to the weekly rate of production in the four or five week period contained or mainly contained in the month or (iii) to the daily rate of production in the month. By choosing different time limits an indefinite number of other possibilities could be defined but for the practical purposes these are the main ones to be considered.

If sales and purchases are regarded as flows then it would seem that the first possibility could be ruled out since the level of the indicators in different months would in most cases depend on the number of days in the month. Consequently for a comparison of flows corrections would have to be made for the varying lengths of the different months.

If the above argument be accepted it might be supposed that the daily rate of sales or purchases would be the best unit to take. While this definition would be satisfactory in cases where production and consumption take place continuously or at regular intervals throughout the month it would not work well in other cases. For the number of Saturdays and Sundays varies from month to month and their incidence would affect the apparent daily rate of flow.

It would seem therefore that on the whole the second possibility, (ii) above, is likely to be the most satisfactory. This means that in principle the fifty-two weeks of the year should be allocated to months and that the average flow of transactions in the different four or five weekly periods so obtained should be reflected in the quantity indicators. For consistency, price indicators should, in principle, be averages for the same periods although in practice they are likely to relate to prices on a particular day within the period.

Even if constructed on this basis, quantity index-numbers will still show variations due to certain recurrent factors such as holidays. If an index is required which does not show the effects of these recurrent factors it is probably best to remove this effect along with other seasonal influences in the index on the lines suggested in section 3 of Chapter VI above.

Indicators for different industries or commodities which cover periods of less than a year show a considerable amount of diversity and so some adjustment to the basic series is usually required before they can all be regarded as comparable quite apart from the question of recurrent seasonal variation. The following different types of series are commonly met with:

1. Weekly averages with a figure for each month which relates to those weeks which fall wholly or mainly within it.

2. Weekly averages based on a different arrangement; for example with the last month of each calendar quarter based on five weeks.

3. Four-weekly totals with a five-week total once (or occasionally twice) a quarter.

4. Four-weekly totals running consecutively through the year and yielding 13 rather than 12 figures each year.

5. Monthly totals.

6. Quarterly totals.

7. Levels, for example of employment, at particular dates.

If the basis suggested above be accepted then (1) provides the ideal type of series and no adjustment to it is needed. Series of type (2) are not ideal by this criterion but, unless the underlying weekly series are available, no adjustment can be made. Type (3) requires that each five-weekly figure can be reduced by one-fifth. Type (4) involves some averaging of adjacent four-weekly totals. It will often be sufficient to allocate eleven of the four-weekly totals to the most closely corresponding eleven months and to derive an estimate for the twelfth month by averaging the two remaining adjacent totals. Type (5) requires adjustment for the number of normal working days in the month. Conditions will differ but in most cases Sundays may be omitted and Saturdays may be counted as half a day. Deductions should not be made for holidays if the average weekly rate for the month is required. Type (6) requires that the quarterly total be first allocated to months and the resulting estimates adjusted as in the case of (5). If x is a quarterly total, a and A are respectively the effective number of working days in one of the months and in the quarter and if n is the normal number of working days in the month, which might be taken as actual working days plus holidays or total days less Sundays and half of Saturdays, then a satisfactory estimate for the month is given by xa/An. Type (7) includes indicators which will have to be adjusted on lines similar to those needed for (6).

5. WEIGHTING

If aggregative index-numbers are written out in their usual form the weights are somewhat disguised. It was recalled however in section 5 of Chapter III that they are all of the form of weighted arithmetic or harmonic averages of price or quantity relatives, the weights being the values of the various commodity transactions in the base year. With complete information all the weights can be calculated from the individual prices and quantities, but in practice the available information is likely to fall short of this ideal. It may be supposed that where fairly detailed national accounts have been compiled the necessary weights for groups of transaction will be known but this will not usually be in sufficient detail to match each available indicator. Similarly the indicators will not usually be available in sufficient detail to match an ideal set of weights and an approximate process of matching weights to indicators must therefore be undertaken.

When there is only a single weight in the national accounts to be applied to a set of indicators it is necessary to subdivide this weight and apportion a part of it to each indicator. If the indicators are exhaustive and mutually exclusive in their coverage it will usually not be difficult to arrive at a reasonably reliable apportionment by combining the base-period quantities of the indicators with information on prices.

It will sometimes happen that there are two or more indicators which could be used to carry a given weight. If the two indicators are unbiased estimates of the movement to be measured and if their errors are assumed to be independent the best indicator to carry the given weight is their weighted arithmetic mean with the reciprocals of their error variances (the amount of information they contain) as weights. In most cases these error variances will be unknown as also will be the correlation between the errors in the different possible indicators but, if they are to be used in combination, some view on these matters must be taken.

Another situation that arises in practice is that a reliable indicator is available for part of a group and a much less reliable one is available for the group as a whole. If no information is available about the movement of the remaining part of the group then there is no means of improving the indicator for the group as a whole. Circumstances may arise however in which an indicator for the remainder of the group which is even less reliable than the indicator for the group as a whole will, when combined with the reliable indicator for the other part of the group, lead to an improved indicator for the group as a whole. In all such cases subjective judgments by the investigator about the reliability of his data cannot be avoided for they will be made implicitly if they are not made explicitly. The use of information is likely to be improved by recognising this fact and by attempting to assess the errors and the relationships between the errors in the data available.

The opposite situation to these is also met with frequently; that is to say there will be cases in which there is no obvious indicator either for a part of a group or for the group as a whole. Where this happens careful consideration must be given to the consequences of various assumptions, for example that the weight of the part of the group in question should be carried by the indicator for the rest of the group or for all groups taken together. It may easily happen that by further search a poor indicator can be found that will give results which are likely to be superior to such assumptions as these.

A problem of an entirely different kind arises if the basis of valuation is throughout to be factor costs rather than market prices. In many cases market prices and factor cost prices differ and it is the former rather than the latter which can be directly observed. If price index-numbers are to be constructed on a factor cost basis it is necessary, of course, to use indicators of factor cost prices but even if only quantity index numbers are to be calculated directly it is necessary to have the weights expressed in terms of factor costs. It is therefore necessary to know the factor cost values of inputs and outputs. Strictly speaking these can only be calculated in the general case with the aid of a detailed input-output table and the calculations are only straightforward if the production functions are of a very simple form. Various approximations are possible however which may be expected to give reasonably good results in practice.

For quantity index-numbers of net output it can at once be seen that if the assumption is being made that inputs are proportional to outputs then the single indicator for any industry can be weighted by the total of factor costs arising in that industry. If however separate indicators are used for gross output and for input then each should carry a weight equal to its factor cost value. If the accumulated factor costs of inputs are relatively unimportant then a good approximation to the index for the industry is obtained if inputs are valued at market prices and outputs are valued at market prices less the indirect taxes per unit levied on the industry.

For quantity index-numbers of final expenditure it is equally necessary to remove the accumulated indirect taxes from the market prices of the various commodities and in principle the same difficulty arises as that which has just been discussed. In practice however it is frequently found that indirect taxation is levied predominantly at a stage which is close to final expenditure. As a consequence it is possible to remove the main items of indirect taxation such as sales taxes, excise and customs duties on consumers' goods, and local rates directly from the market values of specific final purchases. It is then usually possible to find a reasonably satisfactory way of allocating the remaining amount of indirect taxation to the various groups of final expenditure. In this way approximations to the factor cost prices of final goods may be obtained.

6. THE CHOICE OF BASE PERIOD

The function of a base period is to provide a set of values with which to weight quantity relatives or price relatives as the case may be. It is usual to require that the base period should in some sense be " normal " though it is hard to give a theoretical criterion for making a selection. What is important is that as far as possible the economy should be working in such a way that it may plausibly be supposed that its various parts are at least close to equilibrium or at any rate not obviously in violent disequilibrium. These considerations cannot be made very precise and in practice it is hardly possible to do more than attempt to avoid periods which are dominated by an exceptional event or in which the attainment of equilibrium is made impossible by institutional factors. Thus it would be desirable to avoid a year which was dominated by a general strike or by a stock market crash such as took place in the United States at the end of 1929. It is also desirable to avoid a period in which rationing, price control or some other institutional feature has prevented adjustments in prices and quantities.

The consideration just advanced relates to the mutual adjustment of prices and quantities. Prices and quantities may be untypical while at the same time being adjusted to one another as when the supply of a commodity is reduced by some exceptional circumstance and the price rises correspondingly. On the other hand prices and quantities may not be adjusted to one another although one set might not change very much if adjustment were allowed to take place, as might be the case with prices under a system of quantity restrictions on consumers. If the price system of a particular period comes close to reflecting normal price relationships the choice of this period as a base will not affect subsequent quantity comparisons though if, at the same time, the quantities of the period are dominated by restrictions, the same choice will affect subsequent price comparisons.

These propositions can readily be seen as follows. Let the base period be denoted by 0 and the two subsequent periods be denoted by i and j. The Laspeyres quantity index-numbers for i and j relative to 0 are respectively $\Sigma p_0 q_i / \Sigma p_0 q_0$ and $\Sigma p_0 q_j / \Sigma p_0 q_0$ and the ratio of the second to the first of these index-numbers is $\Sigma p_0 q_j / \Sigma p_0 q_i$ which does not involve q_0. On the other hand the corresponding Laspeyres price index-numbers are $\Sigma p_i q_0 / \Sigma p_0 q_0$ and $\Sigma p_j q_0 / \Sigma p_0 q_0$ and their ratio is $\Sigma p_j q_0 / \Sigma p_i q_0$ which does involve q_0.

Difficulties due to the existence of untypical prices and quantities and untypical price-quantity relationships in individual years may be reduced if a series of years are adopted as a base as when index-numbers are related to the average experience of 1935-1939. This procedure, though attractive in some ways, will frequently be prevented by lack of basic information since in the base period sufficient data must be available for weighting purposes. The mass of information resulting from a large scale budget investigation or census of production will often be sufficient to outweigh doubts about the representativeness of the period to which it relates in the choice of a base period.

The choice that is made will also be affected by the kind of comparison that is required. Thus, with the reservations already implied, a frequent change of base is desirable if interest centres on short-period comparisons since this procedure will help to reduce the problem of the appearance of new commodities and the disappearance of old ones. How far the chaining together of such short-period comparisons will help in comparing the present with the more distant past is by no means clear since concentration on the construction of short-period links makes it unnecessary to account for some of the features which ought to be accounted for in making long-period comparisons.

IX

FAMILIAR TYPES OF INDEX-NUMBER AND THE SYSTEM PRESENTED HERE

1. INDEX-NUMBERS IN COMMON USE AND THEIR RELATIONSHIP TO THOSE DESCRIBED IN THIS REPORT

In most countries a number of official index-numbers of prices and quantities are published regularly. Thus it is normal to find the following minimum list:

Price index-numbers:

1. Retail prices (cost of living).
2. Wholesale prices.
3. Prices of special classes of product such as agricultural products.
4. Prices of imported merchandise.
5. Prices of exported merchandise.

Quantity index-numbers:

6. Quantities produced, usually for a restricted number of branches of activity such as manufacturing or agriculture.
7. Quantities of imported merchandise.
8. Quantities of exported merchandise.

These index-numbers are related to those discussed in this Report in the following way:

1. *Retail prices (cost of living).* This index corresponds to the index-number of the prices of commodities (including direct personal services) bought by households. In practice cost of living index-numbers usually refer only to a sub-class of households determined by the occupation or income of the head of the household. Furthermore, in many cases they relate only to a sub-class of commodities as when drink and tobacco or luxuries or services are excluded. In some countries changes in the rates of direct taxes have been introduced into the cost of living index, but this practice has no counterpart in the system discussed here.

A special problem arises because cost of living index-numbers are as a rule used to a greater or less extent in collective agreements between employers and workpeople, and for this purpose are required at frequent

109

intervals (normally monthly) and in a form which does not call for revision or for alternative calculations. Such index-numbers usually relate prices in successive months to an earlier annual base and so involve comparisons of a type discussed in section 2 of Chapter VI.

2. *Wholesale prices.* Index-numbers of wholesale prices in general have no precise counterpart in the system discussed in this Report. As they are usually constructed, the weights of this type of index-number do not have any clearly defined relationship to the actual transactions which take place in the economy. The nearest corresponding index in the present system would be an index of the prices paid for goods actually sold by wholesale trade.

While it is hard to attach any very precise meaning to wholesale price index-numbers in terms of national accounting, it is clear that many of the component index-numbers which are generally presented along with the total index come close to representing index-numbers of the inputs or outputs of various branches of activity. It is suggested that the usefulness of various index-numbers of wholesale prices would be increased if they were so constructed as to relate to well-defined aggregates of commodity transactions and if their weights were determined from this point of view.

3. *Prices of special classes of product.* These index-numbers correspond to price index-numbers of the (gross) outputs of various industries or industry groups and differ from the corresponding index-numbers in the present system mainly on account of differences in industrial classification.

4. *Prices of imported merchandise.* These index-numbers differ from the corresponding index-numbers in the present system in that (a) they are usually based on c.i.f. prices which may include transport services rendered by the importing country and (b) they do not explicitly take imported services into account.

5. *Prices of exported merchandise.* These index-numbers are usually based on f.o.b. prices, but as in (4) they do not take exported services into account.

6. *Quantities produced.* These index-numbers correspond to the net output index-numbers of the present system. They usually relate only to a limited number of industries or industry groups. Factor cost weights are usually employed in their construction and it is usual to assume that inputs are proportional to outputs so that a single indicator can be associated with each part of net output.

7. *Quantities of imported merchandise.* See remarks under (4) above.

8. *Quantities of exported merchandise.* See remarks under (5) above.

It can thus be seen that most of the price and quantity index-numbers which are regularly compiled have a fairly close correspondent in the system described in this Report. The exceptions to this remark are wholesale price index-numbers and many of their components.

2. ALTERNATIVE METHODS OF REDUCING THE MONEY VALUE OF THE DOMESTIC PRODUCT TO TERMS OF CONSTANT PRICES

On the assumption that there exists a time series of the domestic product expressed in current money values it is possible to reduce this to terms of constant prices by division by an appropriate price index; alternatively a quantity index may be constructed. Apart from this, as was shown in Chapter III, the required total may be reached from the side of net products or from the side of final expenditures adjusted for imports and exports. As was also shown in Chapter III, the alternative methods of measuring total product or the price movements associated with it involve operations on the same body of information. The only difference in each case is in the arrangement of the information. Accordingly if the information is complete and if the index-number formulae and the treatment of the many conceptual problems are consistent then there are not in fact several methods, but only one method of obtaining a series of the domestic product at constant prices.

In practice, however, the information available on prices and quantities separately is usually very far from complete and it is necessary, therefore, to make a choice between the various methods of approach. This choice must depend in any case on the nature of the information available.

It is hard to offer any general comments that would be useful in guiding this choice. If good production statistics are available and if the assumption is justifiable that inputs are proportional to outputs then the construction of a set of net output quantity index-numbers is likely to prove a workable approach. If the assumption of proportionality is not justifiable then this approach requires a very great deal more information since it involves quantity information on inputs as well as outputs and also weights for these inputs. A test of this assumption in relation to Canadian data has already been referred to and is given in [8].

The net output approach cannot with any justification be simplified in the above way if the calculation is made to rely on price rather than quantity index-numbers. It is obviously useless to adjust the current money values of the net output of each industry by a general price index of final goods. It is also impossible to make any general assumption to the effect that the prices of outputs of particular industries vary in proportion to the prices of inputs into those industries and so an index-number of net output prices requires information on input and output prices and a full set of weights.

If the final expenditure approach is adopted it is likely that the practicability of using price and quantity information of the kind frequently available will be interchanged. As a rule detailed quantity information on final expenditures is not available and it cannot reasonably be assumed that the quantity of one commodity will move with that of another even within the same group of purchases. In many cases, on the other hand, it is usual to find price information which is much more satisfactory or which could be made so with only a small part of the labour necessary to obtain the corresponding quantity of information. This is in part due to the relative homogeneity of price movements of commodities made by similar processes from similar materials and of the same commodity made by different producers or sold in different regions of the same economy. The first of these homogeneities enables a limited number of price series to carry the weight of a much larger number of commodity purchases while the second makes it unnecessary to aim at completeness of coverage in the price quotations for one commodity which is so necessary in the collection of information on quantities.

3. STILL SIMPLER SHORT-CUT METHODS

In practice it is often found that series purporting to show the movements of real product or real income are obtained by dividing the corresponding series expressed in current money terms by a comprehensive index-number of prices either retail or wholesale. As a short-cut method this approach involves banking very heavily on the price homogeneity referred to in the last paragraph. If the available retail and wholesale price index-numbers contain approximately the same amount of information it can readily be seen that the retail index is almost inevitably to be preferred. If the retail index is a very good one, if foreign trade is unimportant and if there are no exceptional kinds of transaction taking place in the sphere of government expenditure and asset formation it is likely that this method will give reasonably satisfactory results. For even if price movements are considerable those relating to government purchases and asset formation are likely to move in the same general direction as those for consumers' goods. The latter, however, carry by far the largest weight and it will frequently be found that the rather smaller rise in the price of government purchases (and especially the purchase of labour services) goes some way to offset the rather larger rise in the prices of capital goods.

These, however, are bold assumptions and if the method is to inspire confidence it requires a detailed and well constructed retail price index of consumers' purchases. The tendency, however, to bank on price homogeneity which the frequent use of this method displays has some justification. If comprehensive series for quantities are not available it may be better to attempt to patch up this method than to use quantity information which relates essentially to only a few basic commodities.

The steps that might be taken to refine this approach are as follows: First, even without the collection of additional retail price series, it might be worthwhile to recombine the existing series with different weights. This might be possible for one recent year on the basis of comprehensive estimates of consumers' expenditure which might be constructed even if no regular quantity statistics were available. Second, price index-

112

numbers for merchandise imports and exports are usually available and these might be introduced with appropriate weights. Third, it is usually possible to separate out wages and salaries from the other goods and services bought by government. The former could be reduced to constant prices by an index of wage and salary rates while the weight of the latter could be carried on a suitable combination of available commodity prices. Finally, the difficult problem of the prices of capital goods could be handled either by an extension of existing price collections or by attempting to gauge the price movements of construction and machinery. The former could perhaps be approximated by means of information on the volume and value of production in the construction trades and the latter from suitably reweighted average values of import or export classes.

It must not be supposed that these suggestions are likely to lead to wholly satisfactory results or that they can be regarded as anything but a very poor substitute indeed for a complete calculation if one is possible. They can be regarded only as a possible means of improving existing measures of real product in circumstances in which the relevant statistical information is meagre.

X

SUMMARY AND CONCLUSIONS

The ground covered and the conclusions reached in this Report may be summarised as follows:

1. The economic theory of index-numbers sets out a scheme for making price and quantity comparisons based on an assumed knowledge of consumers' preferences or of the technological possibilities open to producers. The empirical information needed to apply this theory is not available. It is, however, possible to measure the price and quantity changes associated with particular collections of commodities. This more limited objective, which in fact forms the basis of actual index-number construction, cannot be improved upon in the existing state of knowledge about consumers' and producers' behaviour.

2. The flows between different parts of an economic system can be divided into commodity (or product) flows and others. A consistent system of price and quantity index-numbers can be based on a knowledge of the former over two or more periods of time. In this system the price and quantity index-numbers associated with total final product are in principle identical with the similar indices associated with total value added.

3. The statement made in the preceding sentence is true provided that a single, consistent, basis of valuation is adopted in constructing all the index-numbers. This basis may be either market prices or accumulated factor costs.

4. Each basis has its uses. The factor cost basis provides a better means of comparing the importance of different industries or products in terms of economic resources used up especially in a country in which indirect taxation and subsidies are unequally spread over different industries and products. Under competitive conditions there will be a tendency for relative market prices to reflect relative marginal utilities and for relative factor costs to reflect relative marginal factor costs. In practice the existence of rationing, monopolies and other forms of market imperfection will to some extent arrest these tendencies.

5. The forms of index-number considered in this Report are the aggregatives, that is to say the weighted arithmetic and harmonic averages of price and of quantity ratios associated with the names of

115

Laspeyres and Paasche. Each of these index-numbers can be expressed as a ratio of value sums whence the numerators and the denominators for component groups are simply added to give the numerators and denominators of totals. The identity price times quantity equals value holds for these index-numbers if a base-(current)-weighted price index is associated with a current-(base)-weighted quantity index.

6. The constituent elements of price and quantity index-numbers are the prices and quantities of individual commodities (or products). It is the movement in these magnitudes that is relevant. In the current as opposed to the base year, a given product may be more or less trouble to produce and may give more or less satisfaction to consumers. Such considerations should only influence the measure of a component of real value added if they change the relationship of inputs from other industries to the output of the industry considered, or if they lead to a change in that output which is not offset by changes in inputs. They should only influence the measure of a component of final product if they lead to a change in the amount of the output considered which finds its way into final uses including a change in stocks.

7. While the external circumstances referred to in the last paragraph should be left out of account in the construction of price and quantity index-numbers, account should be taken as fully as possible of the quality characteristics of commodities. If a commodity is produced in a number of varieties, a single quantity measure cannot, in general, be properly applied to all of them. One method of handling this problem is to treat different varieties separately. In many cases it will not be possible to apply this method because the quality characteristics embodied in actual varieties are subject to constant modification. A more general method is to attempt to determine empirically a set of characteristics in terms of which base-year price-differences can be explained. If this can be done then a means is available of valuing the relevant quality characteristics at base-year prices and in many cases this system of values may be interpolated and extrapolated in order to express the varieties of the current period at base-year prices.

8. The method just described involves the assumption that, in many cases, commodities possess underlying characteristics which provide a better basis for comparison than can be obtained by an enumeration and pricing of varieties. The method can be extended to handle the problems arising from new models and, in some cases, to those arising from new products. Difficulties and uncertainties will inevitably arise insofar as new models or products exhibit important characteristics which lie well outside base-period experience and which therefore can, at best, be only tentatively assimilated, by extrapolation, into the base-period system of values.

9. Differences which are similar in some respects to quality differences arise from variations in the extent to which transportation and other intermediate services are required to meet the needs of different consumers. If these differences are important and if as a consequence of

locational changes or changes in merchandising methods their relative weight is likely to change, then an attempt should be made to record separately the quantity changes relating to the different price categories in the base period.

10. There are a number of ways in which the flow of goods can be routed, conceptually, through the economic system and the data available for the construction of price and quantity index-numbers may approximate more closely what is required for one method rather than for another. With consistent treatment the same results should be obtained however the data are arranged, but in practice the difficulties encountered may be considerable.

11. For some purposes it may be desirable to restrict final product comparisons to goods and direct services and to exclude intermediate services attaching to goods such as are rendered by trade and transport. Comparisons on this basis ensure that physically similar products are valued alike wherever they are consumed and imply that trade and transport are placed outside the production boundary. They are facilitated if the basic data are assembled as in an input-output table with product flows valued at producers' prices and with trade and transport shown as selling their services direct to buyers.

12. Seasonal variations in prices reflect differences in the valuation of superficially similar commodities. Allowance should be made for the fact that out-of-season varieties are valued more highly than in-season varieties and this can be done either by treating supplies available in different seasons as separate commodities or by adjusting the apparent quantities available in different seasons by reference to their normal seasonal value in the base period. Thus if a product normally sells for twice as much in December as it does in June, then a given quantity of the December variety should be reckoned as equivalent to twice as much of the June variety.

13. The problems of quantity variations, new models, new products, differences in location and in distributive services, and seasonal variations all reflect the heterogeneity and changing nature of commodities the varieties of which are superficially alike and are often called by the same names. The methods discussed for overcoming these difficulties all reduce essentially to one method, which consists in attempting to find empirically the factors associated with price differences and in referring the measurements as far as possible to these factors. Under ideal conditions, the quantity measures used would relate to a set of commodities and commodity characteristics each of which commanded a single price in the base period and in terms of which the current-period as well as the base-period commodity transactions could be described. This method is in no sense a novelty, for the problems with which it is intended to deal are central to the comparison of different collections of commodities on the basis of a common system of values. If index-numbers are identified with such comparisons, as they are in this Report,

difficulties arising from the heterogeneity and changeability of commodities may be said to constitute *the* problem of index-number construction, all more fundamental questions being ruled out of practical consideration. It can be seen, however, that quite apart from practical difficulties associated with lack of appropriate data, even such comparisons as are considered here require first that, on the whole, relative prices are systematic and second that the collections of commodities to be compared can be brought, by appropriate description, within a common, ascertainable, system of relative values.

14. Given the construction of a consistent system of index-numbers for the commodity flows in the social accounts, there remains the question of expressing non-commodity flows in terms of constant prices. The treatment appropriate to commodity flows clearly cannot be applied in these cases and all that can be done is to select particular collections of commodities in terms of which to express the purchasing power of various non-commodity totals. The particular collection selected in any given case is necessarily to some extent a matter of choice and cannot be determined uniquely. Except in simplified cases, the condition that the social accounts should balance in real as well as in money terms cannot be made to provide a unique set of deflators for non-commodity flows.

15. The quality of index-numbers must depend to a large extent on the quality of the statistical data available, empirical information about product heterogeneity and the factors with which it is associated, and a skillful use of resources in making the innumerable adjustments and approximations that arise in practice. A summary of such practical problems is virtually impossible but it may be said: first, that each value unit of net output of final product should receive the same attention whether it forms a small part of a large industry or final product group or the whole of a small one; second, that errors that can be corrected should be corrected in spite of the fact that a number of these will remain; and, finally, that it is useless to reject indicators because they are not perfect unless there is something better that can be put in their place.

A LIST OF WORKS CITED

[1] Brems, H., *Product Equilibrium under Monopolistic Competition,* Harvard Studies in Monopoly and Competition, No. 5, Harvard University Press, 1951.

[2] *Brewers' Almanack,* London, Review Press, 1939 edition.

[3] Carter, C. F., W. B. Reddaway and Richard Stone, *The Measurement of Production Movements,* University of Cambridge Department of Applied Economics, Monograph 1, Cambridge University Press, 1948.

[4] Central Statistical Office, *National Income and Expenditure 1946-1953,* H.M.S.O., August 1954.

[5] Court, Andrew T., " Hedonic Price Indexes ", in *The Dynamics of Automobile Demand,* New York, General Motors Corporation, 1939.

[6] Debreu, Gerard, " The Coefficient of Resource Utilisation ", in *Econometrica,* Volume 19, No. 3, July 1951, pp. 273-92.

[7] Divisia, F., *Economie Rationnelle,* Paris, 1928.

[8] Dominion Bureau of Statistics, *Revised Index of Industrial Production 1935-1951,* D.B.S. Reference Paper No. 34, Ottawa, Canada, 1952.

[9] Fisher, Irving, *The Making of Index Numbers,* Boston and New York, Houghton Mifflin Company, third edition, revised, 1927.

[10] Fisher, R. A. and F. Yates, *Statistical Tables for Biological, Agricultural and Medical Research,* Edinburgh and London, Oliver and Boyd, third edition, 1948.

[11] Geary, R. C., "A Note on ' A Constant-Utility Index of the Cost of Living ' ", *The Review of Economic Studies,* Volume XVIII (1), No. 45, 1949-50, pp. 65-66.

[12] Hofsten, Erland von, *Price Indexes and Quality Changes,* London, Allen and Unwin, 1952.

[13] Kendall, Maurice G., *The Advanced Theory of Statistics, Volume II,* London, Griffin, 1946.

[14] Klein, L. R. and H. Rubin, " A Constant-Utility Index of the Cost of Living ", *The Review of Economic Studies,* Volume XV (2), No. 38, 1947-48, pp. 84-87.

[15] O.E.E.C., *A Standardised System of National Accounts*, Paris, 1952.

[16] Rothbarth, E., " The Measurement of Changes in Real Income under Conditions of Rationing ", *The Review of Economic Studies*, Volume VIII, No. 2, February 1941, pp. 100-107.

[17] Samuelson, P. A., " Some Implications of ' Linearity ' ", *The Review of Economic Studies*, Volume XV (2), No. 38, 1947-48, pp. 88-90.

[18] Siegel, Irvine H., " The Generalized (Ideal) Index Number Formula ", *Journal of the American Statistical Association*, Volume 40, 1945, pp. 520-523.

[19] Stone, Richard and Kurt Hansen, " Inter-Country Comparisons of the National Accounts and the Work of the National Accounts Research Unit of the Organisation for European Economic Co-operation ", in *Income and Wealth, Series III*, Cambridge, Bowes and Bowes, 1953, pp. 101-141.

[20] Stone, Richard and S. J. Prais, " Systems of Aggregative Index Numbers and their Comparability ", *The Economic Journal*, Volume LXII, No. 247, September 1952, pp. 565-83.

[21] Stone, Richard assisted by D. A. Rowe and by W. J. Corlett, Renee Hurstfield, Muriel Potter, *The Measurement of Consumers' Expenditure and Behaviour in the United Kingdom, 1920-1938, Volume I*, Studies in the National Income and Expenditure of the United Kingdom, 1, Cambridge University Press, 1954.

[22] Stone, Richard, " Linear Expenditure Systems and Demand Analysis: An Application to the Pattern of British Demand ", *The Economic Journal*, Volume LXIV, No. 255, September 1954, pp. 511-527.

[23] Tobin, James, " A Survey of the Theory of Rationing ", *Econometrica*, Volume 20, No. 4, October 1952, pp. 521-553.

120

FROM THE CATALOGUE

AN INTERNATIONAL COMPARISON OF NATIONAL PRODUCTS AND THE PURCHASING POWER OF CURRENCY (1954)
By Milton Gilbert and Irving B. Kravis

204 pages (demy-8vo)
Cloth-bound, jacket in three colours   **$3.00**   **18/-**   **900 Fr. fr.**

INDUSTRIAL STATISTICS — 1900-1955
176 pages (Crown Quarto)   **$2.00**   **14/-**   **700 Fr. fr.**

●

In preparation :

BASIC STATISTICS OF FOOD AND AGRICULTURE

STATISTICS OF NATIONAL PRODUCT AND EXPENDITURE — 1938, 1947 TO 1955

●

O.E.E.C. STATISTICAL BULLETINS
FOREIGN TRADE BULLETINS

Series I. Foreign Trade by areas (monthly)
This series covers O.E.E.C. Member countries combined and individually, the United States and Canada, Member countries of the sterling area combined and individually, the Overseas Territories of Belgium, the United Kingdom, France, Netherlands and Portugal combined and individually, and other principal countries of the world. It provides a monthly analysis of imports by origin and of exports by destination, showing current values, volume indices, average value indices and terms of trade.

Yearly subscription: **$6.00**   **£2.00**   **2,000 Fr. fr.**

Series II. Foreign Trade by commodity categories and by areas (Quarterly). Gives an analysis of foreign trade by commodity categories and by origin and destination for O.E.E.C. Member countries combined and individually, the United States and Canada.

Yearly subscription: **$4.00**   **24/-**   **1,200 Fr. fr.**

Series III. Foreign Trade in selected commodities (Quarterly)
Gives figures of total imports and exports — in metric tons and in dollars — of some 300 commodities selected for their special importance in European trade.

Yearly subscription: **$4.00**   **24/-**   **1,200 Fr. fr.**

Series IV. Foreign Trade by countries of origin and destination (Six-monthly)
Includes a booklet for each O.E.E.C. Member country, the United States and Canada, giving full quarterly statistics (metric tons and dollars) of foreign trade (total, sections, divisions, commodity groups and about 300 specific commodities, quantities by origin and destination).

Yearly subscription for one country :   **$2.50**   **12/-**   **600 Fr. fr.**

Yearly subscription for 18 countries :   **$45.00**   **£10.16.0**   **10,800 Fr. fr.**

Yearbook :   **$2.00**   **14/-**   **700 Fr. fr.**

O.E.E.C. SALES AGENTS

ARGENTINA
Editorial Sudamerica S.A., Alsina 500, BUENOS AIRES

AUSTRIA
Gerold & Co, Graben 31, VIENNA 1

Sub-Agents :
GRAZ : Buchhandlung Jos. A. Kienreich, Sacktrasse 6
LINZ : Winters Buccchhandlung Hans Fürstelberger, Labdstrasse 49
INNSBRUCK : Wagner'sche Universitkts-buchhandlung, Museumstrasse 4

BELGIUM
Librairie Encyclopédique, 7, rue du Luxembourg, BRUSSELS

BRAZIL
Livraria Agir Editoria, Rua Mexico, 98-B, RIO DE JANEIRO

CANADA
The Ryerson Press, 299 Queen Street W. TORONTO

CUBA
La Casa Belga, O'Reilly 455 HAVANA

DENMARK
Ejnar Munksgaard Forlag, Nörregade COPENHAGEN

FINLAND
Akateeminen Kirjakauppa, 2 Keskuskatu HELSINKI

FRANCE
Presses Universitaires de France, 108, Boulevard Saint-Germain, PARIS 6e

GERMANY
Deutscher Bundes Verlag, G.m.b.H., Bundeshaus, Schliessfach 137, BONN

GREECE
Librairie Kauffman, 21 rue du Stade ATHENS

INDIA
International Book House Ltd., 9 Ash Lane, Mahatma Gandhi Road, BOMBAY 1
Oxford Book and Stationery Co.
NEW DELHI : Scindia House
CALCUTTA : 17 Park Street

IRELAND
Eason & Son, 40-41 Lower O'Connell Street, DUBLIN

ISRAEL
Blumstein's Bookstores Ltd., 35 Allenby Road TEL-AVIV

ITALY
Libreria Commissionaria Sansoni, 26 Via Gino Capponi, FLORENCE

JAPAN
Maruzen Company Ltd., 6 Tori Nichome Nihonbashi, TOKYO

LEBANON
Librairie Universelle, avenue des Français, BEIRUT

LUXEMBOURG
Librairie Paul Bruck, 33 Grand'Rue LUXEMBOURG

THE NETHERLANDS
Meulenhoff & Co. N.V. Importeurs, Beulingstraat 2, AMSTERDAM
« Levering uitsluitend via Uw boekverkoper »

NORWAY
A/S Bokhjornet, Stortingsplass, 7, OSLO

PAKISTAN
Mirza Book Agency, 9-A Shah Alam Market LAHORE

SOUTH AFRICA
Van Schaik's Book Store Ltd., Church Street, PRETORIA

SPAIN
Mundi Prensa, Lagasca 38, MADRID

SWEDEN
Fritzes, Kungl. Hovbokhandel, Fredsgatan 2, STOCKHOLM 16

SWITZERLAND
Librairie Payot, 40 rue du Marché GENEVE

TURKEY
Librairie Hachette, 469 Istikal Caddesi Beyoglu, ISTANBUL

UNITED KINGDOM AND CROWN COLONIES
H.M. Stationery Office, P.O. Box 569, LONDON S.E.1.

Branches at :
EDINBURGH 2 : 13a Castle Street
BIRMINGHAM 3 : 2 Edmund Street
BRISTOL 1 : Tower Lane
MANCHESTER 2 : 39 King Street
CARDIFF : 109 St. Mary Street
BELFAST : 80 Chichester Street

UNITED STATES OF AMERICA
O.E.E.C. Mission, Publications Office Suite 61, 2000 P Street N.W. WASHINGTON 6, D.C.

VENEZUELA
Suma S.A. Calle Real de Sabana Grande 102, CARACAS

Orders and inquiries from countries where sales agents have not yet been appointed may be sent to O.E.E.C., Diffusion and Sales Section, 33, rue de Franqueville, Paris (16e).

PRINTED BY THE O.E.E.C.
2, rue André-Pascal, Paris-16ᵉ

No. 1,131

_____

PRINTED IN FRANCE